$24.55

FOUNDATION DOCUMENTS
OF THE FAITH

FOUNDATION DOCUMENTS OF THE FAITH

EDITED BY
CYRIL S. RODD

T. & T. CLARK LIMITED
59 GEORGE STREET, EDINBURGH

Copyright © T. & T. Clark Limited, 1987

Printed by Spectrum Printing Company Limited, Livingston

for

T. & T. CLARK LIMITED, EDINBURGH

First printed 1987

British Library Cataloguing in Publication Data
Foundation documents of the faith.
1. Creeds—History
I. Rodd, Cyril S.
238   BT990

ISBN 0-56729-138-3

CONTENTS

Preface

THE Jews in the time of Jesus have been accused of being so concerned about exact obedience to the letter of the Law that they misunderstood its spirit and failed to arrive at true religious obedience. Christians from the time of the New Testament may equally be accused of a similar falling away from the true spirit of religion. They have been obsessed with correct belief. It is true, as Professor Pannenberg points out, that the belief centred on the Saviour. 'Jesus is Lord' is generally recognized as the first Christian affirmation of faith. But once the cry is uttered the questions begin. How is he Lord? What is his relation to God the Father? If he is to save us, in what way was he human and divine? Questions such as these were not asked out of speculative curiosity but arose from deep religious concern. Yet the passion for right doctrine led to hostility towards those who differed in their beliefs. Attempts to define orthodoxy were made in order to erect fences against heresy, and all too often they created schism.

The writers of the articles collected here (all but two of which first appeared in *The Expository Times*) seek to present the creeds in a positive way. Each contributor expounds the meaning of the phrases that were crafted in a distant age. Each indicates the continuing importance of the statements in our own day, in an age very different from when they were formed.

Professor Stead shows how the Apostles' Creed 'links our age of unrest with the historic faith of Christendom'. Professor Davies avers that the Nicene Creed makes challenges and demands upon us. Professor Macquarrie firmly declares that attempts to repudiate the Chalcedonian Definition are irresponsible (though he sees no less irresponsibility in a refusal to explore anew today the mystery of God in Christ). Professor Rupp suggests that the Augsberg Confession, which was once a rallying point for Lutherans in Germany, has become changed in our ecumenical age into a meeting place for Protestants and Catholics. Dr Fenlon digs below the phrases of the Tridentine Profession of Faith to present ideas of divine grace and human freedom which are still dear to him and which he finds to be both spiritual and sacramental. Professor Dugmore values the Thirty-Nine Articles as the one link with the reformed Anglican Church of the 16th century that remains after 'the virtual demise of the Book of Common Prayer'. Professor Reid writes on the Westminster Confession with a certain topicality in view of debates within the Church of Scotland, and he is less happy about its continuing use than some of the other contributors; it should, he says, 'recede into the past to which it belongs, and there be given an enhanced because unequivocal place of high honour and limited authority among other historical confessions'. Baptists and Methodists have been somewhat uncertain in their attitude to credal statements, fearing that they may infringe upon individual liberty of interpretation and seeing their doctrinal standards as simply setting out 'the essential message of the Bible', as Principal West and the Reverend Raymond George point out. Dr Bebawi shows how the creed is not dead and fossilized doctrine in the Eastern churches. 'Theology, history and worship are put together in the brilliant way in which the Orthodox liturgy is composed', so that the past becomes a living reality in the celebration of the sacraments, worship and liturgical year, and cannot be separated from the prayers, hymns, and scripture. In a similarly

positive vein Professor Avery Dulles finds great value in modern attempts to restate the faith in terms which are more
immediately comprehensible to men and women today,
although he is well aware of their limitations and would certainly never abandon the historic creeds.

Does this mean that the Apostles' and Nicene creeds are the
necessary and essential foundation of the Christian religion?
Certainly the Niceno-Constantinoplitan Creed is more widely
accepted throughout the various Christian communities than
any other form of words, whether liturgical, doctrinal or ethi-
cal, and modern debate about the *filioque* only broadens this
consensus. It has at the very least unique symbolic significance.

But if we cannot cut ourselves loose from the historic creeds,
how are we to react to the situation within our local churches?
What of those thoughtful and sensitive men and women who
can only repeat the creeds with reservations? And what of those
others, probably more numerous, who have no awareness of
the age in which the creeds were formulated and the nuances of
the phrases they are taking upon their lips, and think they are
committed as Christians to believing the distorted interpretations of the creeds which they have in their own minds?
Professor Pannenberg has helpful things to say about this.

Yet in the end I wonder. Is it not curious that one of the few
certain things which scholars, however radical, however scepti-
cal, are clear about is that Jesus was the friend of outcasts, of
those who did not keep the finer points of the Law? Why then
this passion down the centuries for correct forms of words
expressing the orthodoxy of the 'true believers'?

I leave this as a question to ponder, and add one further comment. Several of the contributors point to the creeds as having
their foundation, in one way or another, in the Bible. Yet the

Bible suffers from almost all the difficulties that have been raised concerning the creeds. It too is the product of a distant age and an alien culture. But there is a further problem beyond language, ways of thought, and social setting: the Bible comprises an extensive literature with diversities of belief and ethics within it. It is not easy to see how, given its very nature, it can provide a basis for any orthodoxy in doctrine, although it plainly provides inspiration for a religious response to God.

Is this whole enterprise of formulating correct belief misguided, then? Should we abandon both the historical creeds and modern credal statements, the ancient creeds because the words no longer mean what we believe, and the modern ones because they are ephemeral and local. Should we go further and see the heart of Christian discipleship not in a doctrine to be believed but as a worship to be offered and a way to be followed? The contributors would not agree. We should pay careful heed to what they have to say.

The Apostles' Creed

THE REVEREND PROFESSOR G. C. STEAD, LITT.D., F.B.A.,
CAMBRIDGE

IT is a fine old half-truth that man is a rational animal. Experience often contradicts it; yet it states an ideal that can in some degree be realized. Other animals may live blamelessly according to their kind; some beasts can even be tender and faithful towards their mates; but only men can believe. And to believe means, among other things, to understand and accept certain propositions and the statements in which they are expressed. No doubt modern students of the mind have insisted that rational activity is only the tip of the human iceberg, poking out from a vast substructure of emotional drives and unnoticed connexions of ideas which give shape to our thought; and they may interpret human rationality as the practice of intelligent behaviour rather than as a detached activity of reasoning, detecting errors, and reaching conclusions. But Christians at least can follow them so far: Christian belief may be condemned as unjustified, as disallowed by the tests of history or science; but it should not be dismissed as irrelevant to the problems of decision and action. Christian behaviour (as distinct from humanist behaviour which some Christians tepidly embrace) can only make sense in the light of Christian belief. Christians behave 'as those who believe and trust in the

Communion of Saints, the forgiveness of sins, and the resurrection to life everlasting'; Christian fellowship, Christian self-discipline, compassion and self-preparation, would not be rational without this belief.

But this involvement makes it difficult to look at the creeds with scholarly detachment; and the difficulty is acute for an Anglican Christian commenting upon the Apostles' Creed. The Book of Common prayer enjoins priests to repeat it twice daily; and for all Anglicans it is presented in the Catechism as the normative statement on Christian belief. No doubt the compilers of the Prayer Book took it to be a formula whose actual wording derives from the apostles; mediaeval churchmen supposed (in error) that they had Augustine's authority for dividing the Creed into twelve articles, each attributed to one of the apostles by name.[1] In Augustine's time, it is true, it had long been thought that a fixed formula was jointly devised and agreed by the apostles; this is clearly stated (among others) by Rufinus of Aquileia, writing about A.D. 404; and he attributes this view to 'the tradition of our forefathers'.[2] No doubt most users of the Prayer Book have never considered any other explanation; for them, the familiar sentences express the mind of Jesus' own chosen disciples.

But anyone who has read at all extensively in early Christian literature is bound to come to a different conclusion. As early as the second century, in writers like Justin Martyr and Irenaeus, there are numerous passages in which the main outlines of Christian belief are formulated; these texts certainly show a general agreement in substance and doctrine, but there is no tendency to reduce it to a fixed form of words; a general conformity seems to have been all that was expected. Scholars refer to these formulations collectively under the title of the 'Rule of Faith' (regula fidei). But it seems unbelievable that this so-called 'rule' with its free variations of wording, should have been repeatedly explained and defended, if at the same time the Apostles' Creed itself were already in existence, approved and used in the Church, but never discussed. For it is the fact that a *statement* of Christian belief which approximately agrees in wording with the Apostles' Creed cannot be found in any surviving writing earlier than A.D. 340, in a letter sent by Marcellus, Bishop of Ancyra, to Pope Julius.[3] It seems overwhelmingly probable that in the early centuries Christians generally trusted their bishops and teachers to express their common faith within a generally accepted convention, choosing their own words to suit the occasion, just as the bishop did in the context of the eucharistic prayer. It was only in the fourth century that this freedom was distrusted and relinquished.

Given that this was the general pattern, we do find one notable exception. The NT itself suggests that at an early date certain very short formulations became current, especially in the confession of faith in connexion with baptism; the earliest we can trace is no doubt the laconic formula 'Jesus is Lord', which is quoted by St Paul (1 Cor 12[3], Rom 10[9]) and is probably implied by the mention of baptism 'in the name of the Lord Jesus' (1 Cor 6[11], Acts 8[16], 19[5]); and a slightly more developed confession is introduced into the account of the Ethiopian eunuch's baptism in Acts 8[37], 'I believe that Jesus Christ is the Son of God', which must reflect early practice even though it is absent from the earliest manuscripts. At all events it seems probable that in the early centuries our creeds developed in close association with baptism, in the formulae delivered to candidates to be memorized and repeated before the ceremony. A fixed formula was no doubt desirable in this context so that (at least within the same city or province) all believers, however simple, could be known to agree on the essentials of their faith.

At the baptism service itself, questions were put to the candidates in roughly the same words; but these questions, like so many liturgical forms, became fixed by tradition; whereas the instructional formula, though still very elementary, had occasional changes made to meet points of difficulty; and the theologians' summaries, as we have seen, enjoyed much greater freedom.

At all events, the first appearance of a formula recognizably akin to our Apostles' Creed is in the baptism service recorded by Hippolytus of Rome in his Apostolic Tradition;[4] Hippolytus was writing about A.D. 215, but his point of view was professedly conservative, so that his liturgy probably represents the practice of some two generations earlier. The candidate is asked:

> Do you believe in God the Father Almighty?
> Do you believe in Christ Jesus, the Son of God?
>> Who was born through the Holy Spirit from the Virgin Mary,
>> And was crucified under Pontius Pilate, and died,
>> And rose again on the third day, living from the dead,
>> And ascended into the heavens,
>> And sat down at the right hand of the Father,
>> And will come to judge the living and the dead?
> Do you believe in the Holy Spirit, and the Holy Church, and the resurrection of the flesh?

Apart from its interrogative form, this wording agrees fairly closely with the version of the Roman Creed set down by Rufinus; and the Greek text of Marcellus, mentioned above, is almost identical with Rufinus, except that it adds the words 'and eternal life'.

Thus in essence our Apostles' Creed derives from the Church of Rome in the second century; a Christian community still predominantly Greek-speaking, as it had been in the days of St Paul, with a solid core of immigrant merchants and tradesmen, reaching out to include numerous slaves and ex-slaves, and a sprinkling of aristocrats, especially among its women members. The poorer classes lived in vast blocks of flats, often of flimsy construction; the slum districts of Naples, as they were in recent times, give a much better idea of the mentality and living conditions of this society than does the romantic picture of the old-Roman austerity which schoolboys used to absorb from Livy. Hippolytus gives a revealing list of professions which Christians were not allowed to practise: brothel-keepers, comedians, charioteers, gladiators, priests (of pagan cults), magistrates, prostitutes, and fortune-tellers can be admitted only if they undertake to relinquish their calling; sculptors or painters and soldiers must promise respectively not to make idols and to take no part in executions; schoolmasters are reluctantly allowed to continue teaching (pagan literature) if they have no other means of livelihood; slaves must obtain their masters' permission to attend, and slave-concubines of pagan masters must promise not to abandon their children and not to consort with other men. The list is a down-to-earth affair, and of course omits the large mass of respectable folk who cause no problems. But the tolerance and self-sacrifice it presupposes is impressive.

For this strangely-assorted community a formula was evolved which followed a simple pattern. The main outline of the Creed is a confession (as we should *now* put it) of the three divine Persons: God the Father Almighty, Christ Jesus the Son of God, and the Holy Spirit; but the second article is considerably expanded by reciting the chief events concerning the life and death and resurrection of Jesus. It is to all appearances a straightforward summary which gives away very little about its origin and intentions. Nevertheless some characteristic features can be outlined.

In the first place, its teaching about Father, Son and Spirit seems in the main to envisage a scheme of three stages of divine action. When God is described as 'Father', the implication is that he is the source of all being, or (in the later expansion) the 'maker of heaven and earth', who acts at the beginning of all things; the Son occupies the central place, from the moment when he was 'born through the Holy Spirit' till the time when he 'sat down' (not 'sits') at the Father's right hand – though admittedly a reference is added to his future coming for judgment; and the Spirit is described in relation to present reality, the Church, and its inheritance, the resurrection. Thus the Creed does *not* state – though of course it does not deny – that Jesus was God's Son from all eternity, or that the Spirit, before Jesus, spoke through the prophets; at each stage one single Person is kept in view, with again one single exception, that Jesus 'sat down at the right hand of the father'.

This tendency to stress the unity of the divine action while playing down the coexistence of the three Persons is one which we know was attractive to the Roman Church in the late second and early third centuries. When pressed to its logical limit, it led to conclusions which were rightly condemned as heretical; we cannot think that the divine action was wholly expressed in three Persons acting successively. Christians do indeed believe that God created us as Father, and redeemed us in Jesus, and inspires us by the Holy Spirit; but the NT makes it clear that Jesus was not an incarnation into which the Godhead was wholly absorbed. We are entitled to call him 'God', and 'Father', and indeed a holy 'Spirit'; but we are taught that he prayed to his Father, he was inspired by the Spirit. Only so could he leave us a pattern to follow. Nevertheless the scheme of three stages has a certain usefulness at a simple level; it avoids some of the perplexities which can arise if we think of the Trinity as a divine committee who must severally counter-sign the cheque for our salvation; or still worse, as a divine hierarchy so arranged that we cannot, like our OT forbears, enjoy direct contact with our heavenly Father, and our access even to Jesus can seem to be blocked by pious exhortations to come to terms with the Holy Spirit.

A distinctive feature of this Creed is that the sonship of Jesus appears to be understood purely in terms of his conception through God's Holy Spirit by the Virgin Mary; there is no reference to an incarnation in its strict sense, as the entry into this world of a being who was previously existent in another sphere.[6] The perspective, then, is that of the Synoptic gospels, especially Matthew and Luke; if there were any powerful influence from John or Paul, it is difficult to see how all the reference to Christ's pre-existence could have been avoided. St John's gospel, we know, was acknowledged at Rome only after some hesitation and delay, and a small party persisted in their opposition. With St Paul the case was different; though distrusted here and there, his major letters were early recognized as important, but not always interpreted with much theological acumen; thus St Clement, writing to Corinth towards the end of the first century, draws upon Romans and 1 Corinthians chiefly to support his appeal for unity and discipline in the church. This pragmatic approach, which became characteristic of Roman churchmen, is certainly not the result of a conservatism and love of order which was ingrained in the Roman character as such: Rome was a cosmopolitan city where religion took many forms, from the formalism of the state establishments to the emotional excesses of the mystery cults; and it accommodated philosophers of all schools. Some of these, and especially some Stoics, expressed the view that speculation was valueless in promoting the good life, and commended self-control and devotion to duty. But there were other factors which influenced Roman Christians to take a similar line; the presence of a sizeable Jewish community, and converts from Judaism within the church, who had already come to terms with the Stoic morality; not to mention local and civic pride, which emphasized the apostolic foundation of the Roman church and saw it as the natural seat of authority.

But Rome also attracted Gnostic Christian teachers, who tried to relate the Christian Gospel to the speculative philosophies of the time, and who also pioneered a more enterprising approach to the work of both Paul and John. In the process, however, they arrived at wildly divergent views of Christ, which often had to be connected by postulating several distinct beings with their own individual names – the Logos and the Only One (*Monogenēs* can mean 'unique', though often translated 'only-begotten') and Christ, who had no part in human flesh, and Jesus, often regarded simply as a man who brought news of his loftier counterparts. Not surprisingly the Roman church had little use for such theories; and the central section of the Creed asserts without effort that it is one and the same Christ Jesus who lived a human life and was exalted to divine honour and will come to judge the living and the dead; the assumption is still that the day of judgment is near; by mentioning those Christians who will be alive when that day overtakes us, it implies that they will not be greatly outnumbered by the dead. The Creed also sets aside the view of Marcion and other Gnostic teachers that the world is a place of suffering and disorder (cf. 1 Jn 5[19]!), and accordingly is the work of an ignorant and limited creator, acting without due authorization from the supreme divinity. In professing our belief in God the Father Almighty we are, in the Creed's original intention, proclaiming our faith in the goodness of the created order; for 'almighty' represents the Greek word *pantokratōr*, better translated as 'ruler of all things'. The lesson was later underlined by adding the phrase 'maker of heaven and earth'.

A much stronger indication of the same concern is found in the concluding phrase 'the resurrection of the flesh'. St Paul's classic discussion would rather have suggested 'resurrection of the dead' (1 Cor 15^{35,42}) or 'of the body' (v. 44); indeed he teaches that we shall be given *another* body, a spiritual body, perhaps resembling our present one in form (the word 'spiritual' certainly does not exclude this, cf., e.g., Lk 24^{37}), but imperishable and fitted out for life in heaven. Understandably, therefore, Paul treats the *flesh* as something adapted only for life on earth (v. 39), moulded like Adam's body out of clay (vv. 47-9) and excluded from the heavenly kingdom (v. 50). In Gnostic thought, however, the flesh becomes something not only mortal but necessarily foul and degraded, a pollution in which the Saviour could have no part, so that he was no longer one with our human race. Moreover, St Paul's depreciation of the flesh could easily be used to support their case. By diverging from Paul and proclaiming precisely the resurrection of the flesh, the Creed affirms that even our physical impulses and affections can be glorified and transfigured; and, by implication, it asserts that total sanctity is possible in our life on earth.

How the Creed developed into its present form is a question for specialists; it appears that an expanded version was developed in the provinces, most probably in France, and was adopted at Rome some time during the ninth century.[7] In the process, some useful additions were made, including 'the Communion of Saints', which at one time was understood – though wrongly – to mean 'fellowship in the *holy things*', and so to supply a much-desired reference to the Sacraments; in fact it points to the fellowship which holds between the 'saints' or faithful Christians in this life and the saints who rejoice in heaven.

More to the point is the question of its relevance and usefulness to us today. One fact which cannot be overlooked is the gulf which seems to have been opened between NT theologians, or an essential school of them, and contemporary liturgists. Whereas the former discard the whole framework of incarnational theology (or in some cases weaken the sense of 'incarnation' so that it means no more than 'divine action among men') the latter seem to have taken pains to assert it in the most artless possible form. Some churchmen, indeed, are active on both fronts, and it calls for some sympathy to understand their frame of mind. Thus the 'Thanksgiving' in the revised Anglican liturgies[8] directly identifies the 'Jesus Christ [God's] only Son our lord' of the Apostles' Creed with the 'living Word through whom [God] created all things from the beginning', who was then 'given', 'to be born as man, to die upon the cross', etc. This leaves us, to all appearances, with the holy Child of Nazareth taken out of time and assisting his father to create the galaxies. Curiously enough, this juxtaposition does not seem to worry the man in the pew, as I think it should; what really bothers him, to judge from recent correspondence, is the suggestion that the words and actions of Jesus may not be reported with literal accuracy in the gospels. While the church learns to live with this ever-widening gulf between its laity and its various brands of professional advisers, there is little doubt that a formula so closely based on the gospels as the Apostles' Creed will retain its usefulness. In phrases of commanding simplicity and economy it links our age of unrest with the historic faith of Christendom.

[1] See the sermon *De symbolo i*, as translated by J. N. D. Kelly, *Early Christian Creeds*, 3. It is not by Augustine.

[2] *Commentary on the Apostles' Creed*, §2 (edited and translated by Dr Kelly, *Ancient Christian Writers*, Vol. 20).

[3] Ancyra is the modern Ankara. Marcellus sought to gain the support of the Roman church by declaring his acceptance of *their* creed. Greek text in Kelly, *Creeds*, 103.

[4] See the edition by G. Dix (SPCK [1937]), 36-37.

[5] Dix, *op. cit.* 24-28, here slightly adapted.

[6] Dr Kelly contests this (*Creeds*, 141-143), arguing that *unicus = monogenēs* ('only') shows the influence of Johannine incarnational theology. I do not find this convincing; one can borrow a word without adopting a doctrine; *gnosis* is a well-known example.

[7] These developments of course involve the Latin text of the Creed, the Greek version having now disappeared, while the Greek church used the so-called Nicene Creed. Our English version stems from the 1549 Prayer Book of King Edward VI.

[8] This comment, originally directed at 'Series II and III', still aplies exactly to three, and approximately to one more, of the six permitted alternative 'Thanksgivings' or 'Ecumenical Prayers' contained in 'Rites A and B'.

The Nicene Creed

PROFESSOR EMERITUS THE REVEREND J. G. DAVIES, D.D.,
FORMERLY EDWARD CADBURY PROFESSOR OF THEOLOGY,
UNIVERSITY OF BIRMINGHAM

THE Nicene Creed belongs to that category of the formularies of the Christian faith that are usually designated conciliar creeds. It was in fact intended to be a standard of orthodoxy and it arose out of the theological controversies of its day. The questions of its origin and date therefore turn upon the identification of the council that promulgated it and of the particular heresy or heresies it was aimed to preclude. Despite its familiar title, the Nicene Creed did not emanate from the first ecumenical council of Nicaea in 325. If the creed of that council is compared in detail with the Nicene Creed the differences are obviously too great to support any direct relationship. These differences concern not only matters of substance but such a host of minor items that it cannot be realistically supposed that anyone would go the trouble of making so many changes. This preliminary conclusion means that the association of the Nicene Creed with the Council of Nicaea cannot be accepted and that the tradition about its parentage is also inadmissible. That tradition, which was widely accepted from the sixth century but seems to have been hinted at in minutes of the Council of Chalcedon in 451, was to the effect that the Nicene Creed was the creed of Nicaea expanded.[1]

The same minutes of Chalcedon, however, do connect the Nicene Creed with the second ecumenical council that met at

Constantinople in 381. They refer to it as 'the faith of the hundred and fifty fathers', whereas the creed of Nicaea was known as 'the faith of the three hundred and eighteen fathers' – the numbers indicating those present at the two councils. Nor is there any strong reason to dispute this attribution, although absolute certainty is impossible since the minutes of Constantinople have not survived. Hence the current practice is to refer to the Nicene Creed as the Niceno-Constantinopolitan Creed, meaning thereby that the beliefs expressed are in accordance with the findings of the first ecumenical council although the actual formulary was endorsed by the second.

This conclusion does not mean that the Creed was invented *de novo* in 381. Indeed, its quotation in the *Ancoratus* of Epiphanius, written a few years previously, seems to rule this out, although it is possible that its presence in the manuscript is due to a later scribe who, finding the wording of Nicaea before him, replaced it with what he thought was the most up to date formulary. However whatever the original text of the *Ancoratus*, the precise lineage of the Nicene Creed remains an unsolved mystery.

The Council of Constantinople met, according to a letter to the emperor prefixed to its canons, 'to renew our mutual regard for each other . . . to pronounce some short definitions, ratifying the faith of the Nicene fathers, and to anathematize the heresies that have sprung up contrary to it'. In the first canon they specified those heresies which related to three topics: first to the doctrine of the Trinity with a corresponding condemnation of all varieties of Arianism; second to the doctrine of the person of Christ with a rejection of the teaching of both Marcellus of Ancyra and of Apollinaris; third to the doctrine of the Holy Spirit with an anathematizing of the Pneumatomachians. Since the creed has these theological debates as its background, some knowledge of them is essential to appreciate the teaching it contains.

By 381 Arianism had almost run its course within the empire – though it was to come back in the form of Semi-Arianism when the northern tribes poured over the frontiers in the fifth century. Arius had taught that the Son of God was a creature, that there was a time when he did not exist, and some of his followers declared him to be unlike the father. At Nicaea the unscriptural word *homoousion* (of one substance) was adopted to affirm that all that the Father is the Son is, i.e. he is completely divine. This is an argument from analogy: just as a mortal child being of the same stuff as his parent is human precisely because his father is, so the Son of God must be divine since he is of the same 'stuff' as his Father. The Nicene Creed therefore preserves this key word as well as the statements that the Son is 'true God of true God, begotten not made' and in this way continues the opposition to the Arian views.

Marcellus of Ancyra – his followers being named in the first canon of Constantinople – had himself been a great antagonist of Arius but he had been led to the opposite extreme. Since the Arians argued from the title 'Son' that he could not have been coeval with the Father, Marcellus asserted that the term only applied to the Word incarnate: the pre-incarnate Word is not Son. This then led him to the further affirmation that after his earthly ministry, the Word reverted to what he was before, immanent in the Father, so that 'God will be all in all'. It is to counteract this that the Creed has a phrase, not in the formulary of Nicaea, viz. 'of whose kingdom there shall be no end'.

That this creed was deliberately aimed at Apollinaris is less obvious. Apollinaris, it will be recalled, denied the full reality of Christ's human nature. As much opposed to Arianism as Marcellus, he sought to turn one Arian argument to the effect that the Son must be a creature since he is changeable whereas God is immutable. Regarding the *nous* or rational soul as the seat of change, Apollinaris posited a human nature without one – this was replaced in Jesus by the Word of God. He further believed this prevented the introduction of an impossible duality into the being of the Saviour. Now it cannot be said that this teaching is explicitly attacked in the creed. Indeed the anathematization of Apollinaris at Constantinople was in general terms and it was not until two years later that the emperor began to issue laws against his followers. Nevertheless at Chalcedon it was said that the words '[was incarnate] from the Holy Spirit and the Virgin Mary' were deliberately directed at Apollinarian teaching to protect the reality of the manhood. It is to be acknowledged with Dr Kelly, that they 'provided the material which, properly exploited, could demonstrate the complete incompatibility of orthodoxy with any of the doctrines to which "Apollinarianism" was applied'.[2] But this does not mean that the words were inserted at Constantinople; they may well have been present in whatever formulary was adopted as a basis and indeed the fact that they could be used against Apollinarianism may well have been one of the reasons for adopting that particular formulary.

When we turn to the teaching on the Holy Spirit there is no questioning that this greatly expanded section was specifically to reject the teaching of Pneumatomachians. Sometimes known as the Macedonians, these heretics who, according to Athanasius had 'left the Arians because of their blasphemy against the Son', could not accept the divinity of the Spirit. In this they were by no means remarkable. Gregory of Nazianzus could say of his contemporaries that 'some consider the Holy Spirit to be an energy, others a creature, others God, and others are uncertain what to call him'. At Constantinople the intention, to quote Dr Kelly once more, was 'to bring the Church's teaching about the Holy Spirit into line with what is believed about the Son',[3] and hence this expanded section. Drawing on scripture, the Creed therefore declares belief in the Holy Spirit, the Lord (2 Cor 3[17f]) and life-giver (Jn 6[63]; 2 Cor 3[6]), who proceeds from the Father (Jn 15[26], cf. 1 Cor 2[12]). The next phrase then refers to the co-worship and co-glorification of Father, Son and Spirit and in so doing reflects clearly one fourth-century orthodox method of argument. This involved the appeal to liturgical practice as providing a norm from which inferences could be made. Thus since the doxology, by then in wide use, ascribes glory to Father, Son and Spirit, the last cannot be regarded as alien from the divine nature. It is true that there is no assertion of the consubstantiality of the Spirit, although identity of honour can be regarded as an equivalent, but it is not so direct and indeed it serves to draw attention to the lack of asperity in the text. The Council sought conciliation; just as Basil himself never in so many words declared the *homoousion* of the Spirit in order not to put off possible allies, so the creed left the door open for further discussion while giving a clear indication of where it stood. The final clause – 'who spoke through the prophets' – renews the scriptural echo (cf. 2 Pet 1[21]).

The section on the Holy Spirit was to receive one further addition in the West at a later date. The words 'and the Son' – in Latin *filioque* – were inserted to declare the double procession, i.e. 'proceeds from the Father and the Son'. This contamination of the original was strongly resented in the East, not only because it constituted a unilateral alteration of an ecumenically agreed formulary but also because it seemed to suggest a dual source of Godhead. In so far as the Father begets the Son, the Father is logically, although not temporally, prior to the Son who therefore derives his being from the Father as source. But if the Spirit, so the argument runs, proceeds from Father *and* Son, the single source of divine being is denied. Whatever the rights and wrongs of this dispute, and it was an important factor leading to the Great Schism, evidence for the change in the West is first found in Spain and from there the use spread to Gaul, but it did not receive approval from Rome until the early years of the eleventh century.

While the Nicene Creed was originally put forward as a standard of orthodoxy, it eventually acquired a liturgical use, finding a place both in the service of baptism and at the eucharist. It may well have been adopted into the baptismal rite at Constantinople from the earliest days of its existence; certainly after 451 it was in regular use and spread from there throughout the Middle East to become the baptismal creed of the main Eastern Churches. It appears to have been introduced into the eucharist first by Peter the Fuller at Antioch in 473 to emphasize the adherence of the Monophysites to the Council of Nicea as opposed, by them, to that of Chalcedon. In the early sixth century, it spread to Constantinople and was adopted in Spain by the third Council of Toledo in 599 as a test for Arians, being recited after the fraction; in the Mozarabic rite it still retains this unusual position. Its recitation was later favoured by Charlemagne and so became habitual throughout the Frankish dominions, but was accepted in Rome only by Benedict VIII in 1014 under the influence of Henry II.

Such being in brief its history and use, there remains the question of its relevance at the present day. There is currently in existence a widespread and somewhat arrogant orthodoxy that stresses the cultural divide between the past of the patristic era and the now of the last quarter of the twentieth century. This divide is said to be so great that it is no longer possible to think the thoughts of our forefathers in the faith: their ideas, their presuppositions, etc., are all so different that their formularies are virtually incomprehensible. If this were really so not only would Christian theology be of necessity cut off from any vital relationship to previous tradition but history itself would become an impossible discipline since ancient documents would on this reckoning be so much gibberish. Of course the style of, say, the Cappadocians, who did so much to crystallize belief about the Trinity, owes a great deal to the Second Sophistic as do their thoughts to Neo-platonism, whereas today many theologians who have not subjected themselves to the discipline of patristic study have possibly never heard of the Second Sophistic and I myself have to admit that I cannot recall having actually met a neo-platonist in the flesh. But as soon as one begins to recognize what the style is and, more important, what categories constitute their thought-world, you do at least have an entrée into that world and the possibility of learning something from it – the wisdom of the past has not all been transmuted by cultural change into meaningless incantations.

Nevertheless there is a problem here that cannot be avoided and I can think of no clearer way of expressing what is involved than by reproducing three sentences from Edward Schille-beeckx's outstanding contribution to a modern view of Christology:

If Christianity really does have universal significance, we are faced with a paradox: on the one hand Christianity will transcend every historical definition of what one may call the essence of the Christian faith; on the other, this essence will only be found in specific historical embodiments of it. Identifying the essence of Christianity exclusively with one historical form and manifestation of it or with one particular definition of Christian belief then becomes impossible. That is the unavoidable consequence of the 'universal significance' of Jesus Christ.[4]

In other words, whatever difficulties there may be for a modern person's understanding exactly what the Nicene Creed means, the formulary itself cannot be regarded as the final word. It represents one stage in the history of Christian belief and this very fact indicates that the faith cannot be settled once and for all beyond the reach of history. Inevitably the Nicene Creed, devised by Greeks interested in questions framed in terms of *ousia*, belongs to its age, but what today is all important is the intention behind it. The Creed presupposes that Jesus of Nazareth – not itself – is the norm and criterion of Christian belief and it seeks to underscore the saving activity of God in Christ. It declares that the definitive salvation from God has been encountered in the man Jesus, that to be in contact with him is to be confronted with God's recreative power. We may not want to use the same terms, but if we do not hold that salvation is in Jesus, we cease, in my view, to be Christians at all and Christian theology dissolves into a miasma of religious studies.

Admittedly 'salvation' is a complex term and its contemporary meaning is not immediately self-evident. However it is germane to our subject to recognize that due to such movements as the Theology of Liberation and Black Theology its social content and social context is more widely appreciated. What is relevant is the way these movements use documents from the past, i.e. the Bible. Here is no naïve biblicism, nor simply an antiquarian interest in ancient records – for them exegesis involves bringing the text into relation with a specific contemporary situation. Similarly it may be suggested that the exegesis of the Nicene Creed should involve its being brought into relation to today's world. What does it mean to say that God is maker of heaven and earth in a world where nature is exploited and abused? What does the salvation that is in Jesus mean for those who live in South Africa or Chile? What are the signs of the life-giving Spirit in our daily lives? The Nicene Creed is not just a set of outdated answers to questions we no longer ask – it challenges and makes demands upon us.

[1] The reader will have recognized by now the extent to which, in this historical section of the article, I am deeply indebted to the magisterial study by J. N. D. Kelly, *Early Christian Creeds* [³1982].

[2] *Op. cit.*, 337.

[3] *Ibid.*, 340.

[4] *Jesus. An Experiment in Christology* [1979], 575.

The Chalcedonian Definition

THE REVEREND PROFESSOR JOHN MACQUARRIE,
UNIVERSITY OF OXFORD

The Way to Chalcedon

There is a clearly discernible path from the Council of Nicaea in 325 to the Council of Chalcedon in 451. Indeed, the Chalcedonian fathers thought of themselves as doing no more than reaffirming the faith of Nicaea. At the earlier Council, the Church had decisively committed itself to the paradox of the God-man. Having long resisted every attempt to deprive Jesus Christ of his humanity, the Church had now equally rejected any diminution of his deity, and declared him to be one in being with the Father. But the paradox of the God-man sets up a tension that is very hard to maintain. Almost inevitably, the pull was toward one side or the other, and in the decades after Nicaea there arose a series of christological heresies. Apollinaris (condemned in 381) visualized the God-man as a hybrid being, a human body animated by the divine Logos, and so neither fully human nor fully divine. Nestorius (condemned in 381) is alleged, perhaps wrongly, to have so separated the divine and the human in Christ as to end up with a dual personality. Eutyches (condemned in 451) opposed Nestorianism so vigorously that he was guilty of the error of letting the humanity of Christ be swallowed up in his deity, so that he is regarded as the founder of monophysitism.

The modern reader tends to find these ancient controversies unreal and boring. But people took their theology very seriously in those days, and the purpose of the summoning of the Council of Chalcedon was to find a way through the conflicting views and to state the faith of the Church with enough clarity to exclude the errors that had been repudiated. Although we may find particular points of controversy wearisome, and although we may be repelled by the personal and political hostilities that were provoked, I believe that a more sympathetic view will discern that beneath much of the obscure terminology, matters of true existential concern for Christian faith, life and worship were being fought out. That very down-to-earth theologian, Hans Küng, has remarked: 'Despite inadequate conceptual aids and the entanglement of imperial politics, the first ecumenical councils succeeded in defending the centre of the Christian message against underestimating either the divine or the human factor. We should be under no illusion. It was not joy in theological speculation or the development of dogma but pastoral concern which led to the definitions of the councils.'[1]

I have said that the way to Chalcedon can be clearly discerned already at Nicaea. But does it begin further back? Is there any discernible path from the NT to Chalcedon, or have we moved into an alien world in which the original confession of Jesus as Lord and Christ has been turned into an artificial metaphysical construct? There are really two questions here. Does the original confession of Jesus as the Christ, as we find it in the NT, already imply belief in the God-man? And if it does, can the way that led to Nicaea and Chalcedon be accepted as a legitimate unfolding of that belief?

I would myself answer both of these questions in the affirmative. They are difficult and complex questions and obviously cannot be fully argued here, but I shall answer them briefly and refer the reader to the works of scholars who have treated these matters in depth.

On the first question, I find convincing the thesis of C. F. D. Moule that a 'high' christology is already present in varying degrees of explicitness in the NT, and that the evidence does not support the view that such a christology was only later evolved through borrowings from extraneous sources.[2] Martin Hengel expresses the matter well when he writes that in christology 'more happened in the first two decades than in the whole of the next seven centuries . . . indeed, one might even ask whether the formation of doctrine in the early Church was essentially more than a considered development and completion of what had already been unfolded in the primal event of the first two decades.'[3]

On the question of the legitimacy of the development from the NT in the direction of Nicaea and Chalcedon, I would say that this was not only legitimate but obligatory. The first simple confessions of faith are made in the moment of a saving experience or in the context of worship. But eventually the believer has a duty to sit down and reflect on these confessions of faith. Are they coherent? If so, are they true? This is where theology begins to supervene, and its work of explicating, sifting, criticizing is indeed obligatory if a faith is being held responsibly. Theology will carry out its work by using the clearest language and conceptuality that it can find, and it so happens that Christianity found hellenistic ideas to hand. At another time or in another place it might have used different ideas, and in fact has done so in the course of its history. But the historical circumstances of Christianity's origins made the use of Greek philosophical concepts inevitable. This did not abolish the faith of the NT but gave it new expression. In Aloys Grillmeier's words, 'The simple original proclamation of Christ can be heard in undiminished strength through all the philosophoumena of the Fathers'.[4]

Leo and Cyril

The Chalcedonian fathers did not need to begin from scratch. Orthodoxy had not been without its defenders during the controversies, and of these, two were outstanding, one in the West and one in the East. Pope Leo I of Rome, whose legates were present at Chalcedon, had in his famous Tome taken issue with the monophysitism of Eutyches, while Patriarch Cyril of Alexandria, who had already died in 444, was the untiring and ruthless enemy of Nestorius. Leo's Tome and two letters of Cyril[5] served, so to speak, as resource documents at the Council, and were approved by it as norms by which its own definition could be judged. 'Peter has spoken through Leo. This is the teaching of Cyril. Anathema to him that believes otherwise.'

But in spite of its admiration for these men, the Council produced its own document and this in fact followed a more carefully guarded middle course between the opposing heresies than either Leo or Cyril. Both of them had, in the heat of argument, made somewhat extreme statements that could be wrongly interpreted. Thus Leo, in opposing Eutyches, had to stress the wholeness and distinctness of the two natures. But surely he was skating on thin ice when he declared: 'The Word performs what belongs to the Word, the flesh what pertains to the flesh. The one is resplendent with miracles, the other submits to insults.' There is a danger here of separating the human and the divine, so that they alternate rather than co-exist in union. There is too a failure to grasp the truth, already taught in St John's Gospel that Christ's exaltation and his humiliation are one and the same. Cyril, on the other hand, in his fear of Nestorianism and its supposed doctrine of 'two Sons', was grudging in acknowledging the distinctness of the natures. He could indeed say, 'We do not mean that the difference of the nature is annihilated by the union', but he could also lend his authority to the view that 'of two natures there has been made a union', which might suggest that after the union there was in fact one nature. It is significant too that the Council did not endorse another letter of Cyril's containing some highly polemical anathemas.

The Council's own definition, therefore, may be taken as a refinement and mediation of the orthodox positions represented by Leo and Cyril. Thus, whatever else may be said for or against Chalcedon, its pronouncement must be reckoned one of the most truly ecumenical in the entire history of the Church. In R. V. Sellers' words, 'In a very real sense, the Council of Chalcedon may be called the place where the three ways (Alexandrian, Antiochene, Western) met'.[6] Grillmeier is even more emphatic: '(In the Chalcedonian formula) as in almost no other formula from the early councils, all the important centres of Church life and all the trends of contemporary theology, Rome, Alexandria, Constantinople and Antioch, have contributed toward the framing of a common expression of faith'.[7] A document with such a background certainly demands to be treated with the greatest sympathy and respect.

The Definition and Its Explanation

Let us now turn to the central part of the Chalcedonian definition of faith:

> We all with one voice confess our Lord Jesus Christ, one and the same Son, the same perfect in Godhead, the same perfect in manhood, very God and very man, the same consisting of a reasonable soul and a body, of one substance (*homoousion*) with the Father as touching the Godhead, the same of one substance with us as touching the manhood, like us in all things, sin except; begotten of the Father before the worlds as touching the Godhead, the same in these last days, for us and for our salvation, born of the Virgin Mary, the Mother of God, as touching the manhood, one and the same Christ, Son, Lord, Only-begotten, to be

acknowledged of two natures (*ek duo phuseōn*), without confusion, without conversion, without division, never to be separated (*asunchutōs, atreptōs, adiairetōs, achōristōs*); the distinction of natures being in no wise done away because of the union, but rather the characteristic property of each nature being preserved, and concurring into one person and one subsistence (*eis hen prosōpon kai mian hupostasin*), not as if Christ were parted or divided into two Persons, but one and the same Son and Only-begotten God, Word, Lord, Jesus Christ.[8]

Obviously this is a densely packed statement, where every word and phrase needs to be examined. The authors themselves claimed that these things have been 'formulated by us with all possible care and exactness'. It is clear then that our 'explanation' can touch on only a few points, but I believe that they are vital ones for understanding the definition as a whole.

We begin by considering four basic terms in the definition: *ousia, phusis, hupostasis, prosōpon*. The first three of these are especially confusing, for not only did their meaning vary, worse still, these meanings overlapped. Thus each of these three terms could and did have at least three distinct meanings, and any one of the three terms could and sometimes did bear any one of the three meanings! What then were the three meanings?[9] They were: (1) 'substance', understood as the underlying reality of anything; (2) 'essence', understood as the basic properties that make something one thing rather than another; and (3) 'subsistence', in the sense of a distinct, concrete, existing entity. The Chalcedonian fathers, of course, were making a strenuous effort to use language carefully, and in the definition one could say that roughly *ousia* was used for 'substance', *phusis* for 'essence', and *hupostasis* for 'subsistence'. But the variant meanings must obviously have been resonating in their minds, and this, I believe, was no bad thing, for it introduces into the definition an element of flexibility in interpretation and delivers us from a frozen rigidity. In particular, I think that our traditional English translations, 'substance', 'essence', and 'subsistence', are far too static and that the definition only comes alive and begins to have some plausibility if we can understand it in a much more dynamic way. There is nothing sacrosanct about these traditional translations and the ways of understanding which they carry with them – in some cases they were quite misleading.

In the case of *ousia*, which occurs in the definition as a component of the term *homoousion*, I think that the simple and more accurate translation, 'being', is far more illuminating than 'substance'. It is in fact being used in modern liturgical versions of the Nicene Creed, in which Christ is described as 'of one Being with the Father'. This language can be understood in a lively way. It refers not to some metaphysical substrate, but to the no less ontologically conceived reality of spiritual and personal being. The being of God is creativity, love, freedom – and on the level of the finite these also constitute the being of man when he becomes truly man and manifests the image of God. Jesus Christ is the Mediator because as man he is one in being with the human race, but as the man in whom humanity has been realized, he is also one in being with the Father.

Jesus Christ is the particular being, the concrete historical instance, of the union of the divine and the human. That he is a living personal being is obscured by the use of a term like 'subsistence' or the expression 'hypostatic union'. We should speak rather of the personal union or the historical union. The word *hupostasis* is in fact coupled with the word *prosōpon*, and though the latter did not mean 'person' in the full modern sense, it did convey the idea of a fully concrete appearance or manifestation.

But, as I have suggested in an earlier writing,[10] the key term in the definition is *phusis*, and this is perhaps borne out by the fact that we refer to it as the two natures doctrine. It we take *phusis* to mean 'essence', understood as a fixed stock of characteristics, then it would be very hard to make sense of two natures concurring in one subsistence. But here we may remember that the Greek word *phusis* was originally a very dynamic term, with some such meaning as 'emerging'. Even in Aristotle, according to Christopher Stead, *phusis* could mean 'an immanent formative principle that controls the development of living things'.[11] The Latin equivalent *natura* had originally a similar dynamic meaning. It is formed from the future participle of the verb *nasci* , to be born, so that *natura* meant everything that might arise or be born out of something. In the case of human nature, it is obvious that this is not a fixed essence, everywhere uniform and settled, but something that is coming to be as man strives to find his authentic humanity. This is not only a modern idea of humanity, for it is found in ancient writers also. Theophilus of Antioch and Athanasius of Alexandria are good examples of early Christian thinkers who thought of man as having been called out of nothing to rise through successive stages of being to participation in the divine nature. We must think of the divine nature as also dynamic, for if God's being is love and creativity, he must go out from himself in the self-communication of his word. And how will that word communicate with the creatures except through a human person who can both receive and express it? So the idea of the two natures concurring in the one person of Jesus Christ makes very good sense, if we conceive the language in a dynamic way.

I have indicated that such dynamic ideas were not foreign to the Greek mind, and are not just modern importations. They must have been present in the minds of at least some of the Chalcedonian fathers, though no doubt different members of the Council understood the formula in different ways. We have already seen the variations of meaning in the basic terms, though certainly Chalcedon was also instrumental in sorting out these meanings. Still, as Stead reminds us, 'there is no question of an orthodox or a heretical use of *ousia* . . . it was used in a wide variety of senses which the users themselves largely failed to recognize'.[12] On the other hand, Grillmeier points out that for Apollinaris *phusis* is 'by no means the static abstract *essentia* . . . but self-determining being'.[13] I am not, of course, claiming that the interpretation I have given here reproduces what even some members of the Council may have understood by their formula, though it is possible that it may have done so and it is compatible with their language. But one is not trying to reproduce exactly the thought of the past (if that is indeed possible). When that thought has been expressed in a text, it acquires its own independence and creativity, and one has a duty to put upon it the most plausible interpretation that it will bear.

We pass from the terms just considered to the four negative adverbs: *asunchutōs, atreptōs, adiairetōs, achōristōs*. It seems to me that these did, with considerable success, steer theology on its dialectical way between one-sided exaggerations. But I am not proposing to examine them in detail, but simply to note that their negative form prevents the definition from becoming too rigid and precise. These negative words hold open the possibility of further development and also preserve something of the mystery that must be attendant on any talk of God and his relation to mankind – a mystery which is threatened if we try to imprison God and his action in too precise concepts. It was the Chalcedonian formula that Karl Rahner had in mind when he wrote: 'The clearest formulations, the most sanctified formulae, the classic condensations of the centuries-long work of the Church in prayer, reflection and struggle concerning God's mysteries: all these derive their life from the fact that they are not end but beginning, not goal but means, truths which open the way to the ever greater truth.'[14] Chalcedon sought to settle some of the disputes of earlier times, but it set christology on a dialectical course that allowed for new developments, as is indeed amply shown by the remarkable flowering of Byzantine christology in the subsequent centuries.

Some Criticisms

We have seen that Chalcedon united in a remarkable way several streams of theology, and it continued to guide christological reflection in mainstream Christianity, even until well after the Reformation. It is true that from the beginning some churches in the East had been dissatisfied, and they have remained monophysite to this day. But the radical criticism of the Chalcedonian formula has arisen only in modern times. There are, I think, three main criticisms. It has been held: (1) that the two natures doctrine is logically incoherent; (2) that the whole approach of Chalcedon is abstract and metaphysical, and so misses the existential and soteriological significance of Christ; (3) that the categories of Greek philosophy used by the Council have distorted the biblical faith in Christ and imprisoned it in an alien conceptuality. All of these criticisms were already being made in the nineteenth century, and we shall consider them in the forms in which they were stated by three outstanding theologians of that period.

Schleiermacher, whose own christology still repays study, certainly believed that Christ was in some sense both human and divine, but he did not think that this could be expressed in terms of two natures concurring in one person. His logical critique of Chalcedon is brilliant.[15] How, he asks, can one speak of

a 'divine nature' and a 'human nature', as if there were a genus
'nature' of which the divine and the human are specific determinations? Even worse, how can one 'in utter contradiction to
the use elsewhere, according to which the same nature belongs
to many individuals or persons', speak of one person's sharing
in two quite different natures? This is to reverse the roles of
universals and particulars.

Schleiermacher's criticism would, I think, be unanswerable
if 'nature' were taken in the sense in which he and many other
theologians have taken it – as a fixed universal essence. For
then to say that one person possessed two different natures each
in its entirety would be much like saying that the same animal
was at one and the same time wholly a dog and wholly a cat. But
if 'nature' is understood in the dynamic sense which I have
attributed to it above, then I think that Schleiermacher's
criticism falls to the ground.

The second type of criticism is well represented by Ritschl,
though it had already been hinted at much earlier by
Melanchthon and has continued in Bultmann and others in a
different form. In Ritschl's view, christological statements are
value-judgments. They express the fact that in Christian
experience Christ has the value of God; in and through him we
experience the saving power of God. The formula of
Chalcedon, on the other hand, is a judgment belonging to the
sphere of disinterested scientific knowledge[16] – or, better,
pseudo-scientific knowledge, for it is a metaphysical statement,
and Ritschl would not allow the possibility of metaphysics. But
elsewhere he argues that all our scientific judgments are accom-
panied by value-judgments. 'Without interest we do not trouble ourselves about anything.'[17] Here he would seem to have
proved too much, for it would follow that the Chalcedonian
formula too, in spite of its 'scientific' language, must embrace

value-judgments and must be concerned with existential and soteriological questions, as we indeed maintained near the beginning of this article. So Ritschl's criticism fails, though it may well be conceded that the language of Chalcedon conceals its existential dimensions. Still, one could bring against Ritschl the counter-criticism that responsible value-judgments cannot evade an inquiry into the status and being of the entity to which they ascribe value.

Criticism of the specifically Greek character of Chalcedon found expression in Harnack, and everyone knows his famous remark that 'dogma in its conception and development is a work of the Greek spirit on the soil of the gospel'.[18] Harnack did in fact acknowledge that the Church was under the necessity of stating its beliefs as clearly as possible, but he believed that the Hellenistic thought-forms which it employed were a distorting influence and that the rise of christological dogma was a particularly unfortunate departure from the original Gospel. How we shall judge this criticism will depend on whether or not we have been persuaded by the claim made earlier in this article that christological dogma was a legitimate development from the NT. But we should bear in mind another point, overlooked by Harnack and by many other critics of the alleged Hellenizing of the Gospel. Just as Christianity took over from Jewish thought terms such as Messiah and profoundly changed their meaning in the new Christian context, so it was with terms borrowed from Greek philosophy. Christian doctrines were not conformed to the mould of already existing terminologies, but terms already available were adopted into Christian discourse and given new meanings.

However, I am not saying that the particular terminology of the Chalcedonian definition must remain as a permanent feature of Christian theology. It has indeed acquired a classic status, but it also has the limitations of a given historical and cultural origin, and the very principle of incarnation would demand that christological teaching should find ever new embodiments in fresh cultural forms.

Chalcedon Today

In the newest American revision of *The Book of Common Prayer*, the Chalcedonian definition, together with the Athanasian Creed, the Preface to the Prayer Book of 1549, the Articles of Religion and the Chicago-Lambeth Quadrilateral, have been placed in a section entitled 'Historical Documents of the Church'. These have been landmarks on the way by which the American Episcopal Church has come to where it is today.

I think there is much to commend this way of looking on Chalcedon. We receive it with gratitude and loyalty as a formative document which has given direction to the Church. But in continuity with its insights, we have to wrestle with the christological problem in the context of the problems and thought forms of our time. If it would be irresponsible to repudiate Chalcedon, it would be equally irresponsible to take it over thoughtlessly or to think that it excuses us from the task that must be taken up by every generation of Christians, the task of exploring and proclaiming anew the mystery of God in Christ.

[1] Hans Küng, *On Being a Christian* (London [1977]), 448.

[2] C. F. D. Moule, *The Origins of Christology* (London [1977]), 6.

[3] Martin Hengel, *The Son of God* (London [1976]), 2.

[4] Aloys Grillmeier, *Christ in Christian Tradition* (London [²1975]), 555.

[5] Texts in C. A. Heurtley, *De Fide et Symbolo* (Oxford [⁴1889]) and translations in the same author's *On Faith and the Creed* (Oxford [²1886]).

[6] R. V. Sellers, *The Council of Chalcedon* (London [1961]), 203.

[7] Grillmeier, *op. cit.*, 544.

[8] Text and translation in Heurtley, see note 5.

[9] Cf. Sellers, *op. cit.*, 138, n. 7.

[10] J. Macquarrie, *Principles of Christian Theology* (London [²1977]),297.

[11] G. C. Stead, *Divine Substance* (Oxford [1977]), 71.

[12] Stead, *op. cit.*, 224-5.

[13] Grillmeier, *op. cit.*, 334.

[14] Karl Rahner, *Theological Investigations*, I (London [1961]), 149.

[15] Friedrich Schleiermacher, *The Christian Faith* (Edinburgh [1928]), 392-5.

[16] Albert Ritschl, *Justification and Reconciliation* (Edinburgh [1900]), 398.

[17] Ritschl, *op. cit*, 204.

[18] Adolf von Harnack, *History of Dogma*, I (London [1894]), 17.

The Augsburg Confession, 1530

PROFESSOR GORDON RUPP, F.B.A., D.D.,
CAMBRIDGE

THE Augsburg Confession is the first, and one of the most impressive, of the confessions evoked by the Protestant Reformation. Like the confessions of the early centuries, it arose from a particular crisis in the Church, and is indeed so rooted in particularity, in the complex relations between Pope, Emperor, German Princes and the newly named Protestants that few, on the day of its first utterance, could have guessed that it would have ecumenical significance, or would after four centuries still need to be taken seriously as of more than antiquarian significance.

The Diet of Augsburg, summoned by the Emperor Charles V in 1530 came at a time when a break in the political clouds offered a chance to deal with the German situation, and though the Emperor himself was an uncompromising foe of the Reformers, his invitation was irenically worded and gave some hope that at least some sort of compromise might be agreed which would keep the peace in Germany, menaced as it was by the imminence of the Turkish invasion. Luther, as an outlaw of the Empire, could not attend, and had to wait and fidget in the Castle Coburg, writing tracts and encouraging his friends by correspondence. Among the Protestant princes, the leadeers were the young Duke John Frederick of Saxony, and the more aggressive Philip of Hesse, who at this time was entangled in several political ploys and contemplating joining Zwingli's projected alliance of anti-Roman cities. The Lutherans, however, were averse from any entanglement with the Swiss, and even Strasbourg was to be forced by Lutheran intransigence in the matter of the eucharist, to join with three smaller cities into making its own confession. Moreover such was the antipathy of the Lutherans to the radicalism typified by the Anabaptists that it became evident that they were prepared to denounce the radicals while stressing the irenical nature of their own theology, so that Melanchthon could claim that his confession was genuinely catholic and could indeed be accepted by Roman Catholics if they were willing to rest on the Holy Scriptures and the early Fathers. For it was upon Philip Melanchthon that the weight fell of preparing a Protestant statement of faith, ably seconded by the lay ex-Chancellor of Saxony, Gregory Bruck and a band of theologians and preachers. Maurer has shown that in preparing a theological statement, Melanchthon went back to a confession of faith written by Luther in 1528 in which he affirmed his faith in the ancient Trinitarian and christological tenets of the first centuries. It was also deeply affected by a great distinction which Luther had already drawn in 1520 between those doctrines which were of the heart and essence of the Gospel, and about which there could be no compromise, and the non-essentials and practical abuses, which were in a different category. Melanchthon had as a basis a series of articles worked out in earlier discussion at Torgau and Schwabach, and when he got to Augsburg, got hold of a copy of over four hundred articles in which the Catholic publicist John Eck had arraigned Protestant doctrines of all kinds, but mainly from the writings of Luther and Zwingli.

It has never been seriously questioned that Philip Melanchthon was the chief author of the Augsburg Confession: he continued to treat it as his own document, even after it had attained a semi-official status, and it was he who after a

Catholic confutation had been issued, wrote a long and beauti-
ful theological document which was his 'Apology'. The first
part of the Confession, concerned with the articles of faith
begins with an affirmation, following the Nicene Fathers, of
the Unity and Trinity of the divine nature and condemns modern as well as ancient forms of heresy concerning it. It is
followed by an affirmation of the doctrine of Original Sin
which has befallen all men since the Fall of Adam by which
men are born 'sine metu Dei, sine fiducia erga Deum, et cum
concupiscentia' ('without the fear of God, without trust in him
and with concupiscence'). This is followed by a christological
affirmation along traditional lines, and this in turn by the article
'Of Justification'. This sandwiching of anthropology between
theology and christology is a sound and striking feature of the
opening of the Confession. The limpid sentence about justification supports a forensic view, appealing to Romans 3 and
4, and its succinctness draws attention to the limitations of confessional theology – it was to draw an alarmed letter from John
Brenz to Luther asking him what had become of the doctrine of
Christ's inward presence within the soul. There follows an article on Word and Sacrament as the means whereby the Gospel
is objectively applied to men, and a condemnation of the
Anabaptists who rely solely on the Spirit and the inward
Word.

1530 was a long way from the polemic and paradoxes of the
early 1520s and against the charge by Catholic publicists that
the Reformers were antinomian, and against the aberrations of
some Anabaptists, it was now necessary to include Article VI
which stresses that faith must issue in good works 'propter
voluntatem Dei' ('because it is God's will'). Article VII contains
the most famous definition of the Church as a 'congregatio
sanctorum in qua evangelium recte docetur et recte

administrantur sacramenta' ('a congregation of saints in which the Gospel is rightly taught and the sacraments rightly administered') though there have been those who have seen in it that over stress on the importance of 'pure doctrine' which some have thought to be a weakness haunting Lutheranism. It is said that for the unity of the Church 'satis est consentire de doctrina evangelii et administratione sacramentorum' ('it is sufficient to agree concerning the doctrine of the Gospel and the administration of the sacraments'), though there is still discussion, in our ecumenical age, of the content of 'satis est'. Baptism and the eucharist are dealt with with minimum verbiage and the Real Presence affirmed, with other questions left. Confession is retained in Article XI. There follow articles on repentance, the use of sacraments and ecclesiastical orders and rites, on civil affairs, on the return of Christ, which take up points in earlier articles and avoid misunderstandings and misrepresentations. The long and careful article on Free Will (XVIII) guards against one such misunderstanding when it affirms that fallen man has some freedom in regard to civil righteousness and Pelagianism, ancient and mediaeval is condemned. Article XX now greatly expands what had been said about Good Works and sets them in the context of the late mediaeval Church and its practical abuses.

To these practical abuses, which the Reformers claimed were novelties brought into Christianity by the mediaeval Roman Church, the second half of the document was addressed. Behind it is a good deal of debate between the advisers and the Emperor on the one hand and the authorities in Rome, as to whether, for the sake of peace, the reformers might be given practical concessions, in the matter of Communion in both kinds, in the marriage of the clergy and in release from monastic vows. Following these articles, discussion of these so called 'Abuses' was to be very important in the next decade which saw the formation of the Protestant Schmalkaldic League and in conversations with the Kings of England and France. There is a long final discussion about episcopal order and the character of jurisdiction which was the one point where it seems Luther and Melanchthon were prepared to compromise to the extent of being willing to allow the German bishops to go on ruling, as long as the Reformers were allowed freely to preach the Gospel within their territory. The Emperor would not allow the document to be read at a plenary session of the Diet but it was read in German on 25 July, 1530 between four and six in the afternoon in the Chapter House of the bishop's palace. A Latin copy was handed over, but no original copy of either version has survived. It is clear that many Catholics were staggered at the moderation and reasonableness of this Protestant doctrine though the Catholics immediately began to write its confutation, a copy of which was refused to the Reformers.

Whether Luther saw a first draft, and when he saw the whole document is not certain, but he was generous in his praise:

> It pleases me very well. . . . I have nothing to improve or change in it nor would it be fitting for me to do so for I cannot walk so delicately.

Only when argument continued and it was rumoured that Melanchthon might make dangerous concessions did he show some anxiety, but to others like Conrad Cordatus, Luther expressed his joy:

> I am tremendously pleased to have lived to see this moment when Christ by his staunch confessors has been publicly proclaimed in such a great assembly by means of this really most splendid confession.

So the Confession stood, and soon became a rallying point for the Lutherans in Germany, the indispensable theological certificate for admission to the Schmalkaldic League. And its influence became clear in the negotiations in the 1530s with English theologians, by reason of which very important sections of the Confession were to permeate those English confessional documents which culminated in the Thirty-Nine Articles. There were very important omissions in the Augsburg Confession however, called forth by its irenical intention and the historical context, the two most important being a discussion of the authority of the Papacy, or of Holy Scripture, not least in relation to Tradition. Thus even among the Lutherans it had to be supplemented by other confessional statements.

None the less, as Rudolf Hermann showed in a famous essay, this document, so rooted in particular circumstances became a great confession, set for the rising and falling of churches and nations. The recent suggestion that at its fourth centenary in 1980 the Roman Catholic Church might as an irenical gesture, in the true spirit of 'De Ecumenismo' recognize the Augsburg Confession as a true Christian Confession, is being taken seriously by Roman and Lutheran theologians and has already sparked off a luminous debate in writings and in conferences, proof if it were needed that the document is still 'relevant' because it deals with issues of abiding significance. And, though it was written by theologians as a theological document, we may not finally forget the part played by the laymen at Augsburg – evidence of a new partnership between spiritual and temporal men, between godly magistrates and godly princes and the preachers of the Word. Standing side by side they witnessed a good confession, and the utterance justified the proud claim which was printed on its title page when it went out to the Christian world:

Et loquebar de testimoniis in conspectu Regum et non confundebar

They shall speak of thy testimony before Kings and shall not be put to shame.

The Tridentine Profession of Faith

THE REVEREND DR DERMOT FENLON,
BURY ST EDMONDS

AT the heart of the religious divisions of the sixteenth century there can be discerned two questions. How does God communicate himself to fallen humanity? How does fallen humanity respond? Each of these questions is reducible to single question: how is salvation transmitted within the created community of the redemption which is the Church of Christ?

From the outset, those remaining in communion with the Church of Rome expressed unease about the Protestant doctrine of man. Erasmus, writing in 1524, insisted upon the liberty of the redeemed Christian will. Luther, in his reply *On the Enslaved Will*, outlined an anthropology of perpetual bondage to the dominion of concupiscence.

In the view of Catholic critics, the Protestant reformers underestimated the effects, within human nature, of divine grace. The conviction that their teaching contained an implicit Manichaeism was pithily expressed by Thomas More:

> For this execrable heresy maketh of God the cause of all evil, and such cruel appetite, as never tyrant nor tormentor had, ascribe they to the benign nature of almighty God.[1]

What was at stake, in this analysis, was the image and likeness of God, his 'benign nature', communicated through his

Son in the creation, incarnation and redemption of humanity.

The anthropology of the redemption was, therefore, among the first of the issues to engage the Council of Trent, which assembled in 1545. When the Council closed, in 1563, there existed a body of teaching covering the issues raised by the Protestant reformers, together with a series of decrees for the pastoral and spiritual reformation of the Catholic Church. Before it disbanded, the Council called for a Profession of Faith to be drawn up and to be made binding upon all who held a cure of souls.

The publication of the Formula was hastened by concern for the integrity of the faith taught in the Catholic universities of Europe. At Innsbruck, the experience of the Jesuit St Peter Canisius convinced him of the need for an immediate formula of profession to be made by the teaching staff of the Church's universities. At Rome, St Charles Borromeo and Cardinal Simonetta ensured that Canisius got a hearing. Pius IV, on 13 November, 1564, provided the text which became established as the *Professio Fidei Tridentina*. Thus the unity of faith animating Pope and Council found expression in a single credal formula.

The Profession of Faith condensed the teaching of Trent in a series of declarations opening with the Nicene Creed. Together with this Creed were affirmed the 'apostolic and ecclesiastical traditions' of faith, along with sacred scripture as taught by the Church 'to whom it belongs to decide upon the true sense and interpretation of the sacred Scriptures'.[2]

In this statement there was engaged the first, and decisive, step in resolving the question of how God communicates his revelation to humanity. Here was decided the question of authority on earth to teach in his name. The Council of Trent, in declaring itself to be a duly convened ecumenical Council, was referring its authority to the continuing action of the Holy Spirit guiding the Church in the transmission of revealed truth. The Church, in this perspective, was the repository of divine revelation. Revelation was understood to be the Word of God, the Gospel, a body of orthodoxy entrusted by Christ to his apostles, to be preached. The Gospel, preached: not by scripture alone', but a definite teaching of faith and morals, a *traditio* of saving truth, orthodoxy and the sacramental means of living it, communicated with the scriptures under the guidance of the Holy Spirit. Scripture and the Tradition were here presented as mutually illuminating each other under this same guidance, and were to be received within the faith proclaimed by the Church. Thus, through his Church, did God's love communicate itself to fallen humanity, and invite, in return, a response of love grounded in faith, penitence and hope in the divine promises. Here the disputed questions of free will and grace, of original sin, of sacraments and sacrifice came to the fore.

The Tridentine Profession of Faith followed the Council in affirming the existence of seven sacraments instituted by Jesus Christ, and 'necessary for the salvation of the human race, though not all are necessary for each individual person'. These seven sacraments, baptism, confirmation, eucharist, penance, extreme unction, holy orders and matrimony, were recognized as conferring grace.

Illaque gratiam conferre: with this declaration on the saving power of the sacraments we find ourselves at the heart of the Tridentine teaching on regeneration, a teaching summarized in the observation: 'all true justification either begins through the sacraments, or once begun, increases through them, or when lost is regained through them'.[3] The Profession of Faith, in requiring assent to the teaching of the Council on original sin and justification, was recalling a doctrine which not only affirmed the emancipation of the will from bondage to concupiscence, but a doctrine which emphasized the engagement of the Christian in a lifelong battle against concupiscence: a battle which might be lost or gained according to the free consent of the will. Not by accident did the Council describe justification as a 'renovation of the interior man through the *voluntary* reception of grace'.[4]

The Tridentine teaching on justification rests on the distinction between concupiscence and sin, a distinction which goes to the root of the difference between Trent and the early Protestant Reformers. When the Council declares that concupiscence 'is left for us to wrestle with' and cannot harm those who do not consent but 'manfully resist it by the grace of Jesus Christ' it rescues the Augustinian understanding of *libertas*, and expounds an anthropology of the redemption centred on the mobilization of the will by grace.[5] Through the divinely infused virtues of faith, hope and charity, the redeemed soul, in the teaching of Trent, was united with Christ and in him, so as to become a living member of his body and capable of cooperating in the redemption. From this new life of grace, free will might yet depart by assent to mortal sin. From the ensuing death of soul, repentance and absolution would bring renewed justification by the grace of Christ, and with the infusion of Christ's virtue into the souls of his members, fresh progress in works done 'in God' and by his grace truly meriting eternal life. Such were the fruits of God's justice, infused into the soul through the merits of the Redeemer. As the branches inhered in the vine, so were the members truly united with their head. In this union was constituted the mystery of the Church. In the eucharist this mystery found its focal point and climax.

The Tridentine Profession of Faith declares that 'in the Mass there is offered to God a true sacrifice, properly speaking, which is propitiatory for the living and the dead'. In this one sentence we find the summation of Trent's response to the pivotal issue of the Reformation. Luther, writing in *The Babylonian Captivity* (1520) declared:

> God does not deal, nor has he ever dealt with man in any other way than by the word of his promise. So too we can never have dealings with God in any other way than by faith in that word of promise ... A man can draw fruit from the Mass only through his own faith, and cannot bestow it upon another.[6]

Dr Francis Clark, quoting this passage, finds in its 'radical opposition of inner "word" to sacramental "work" . . . the theological key to the storm of hostility to the Mass which swept across Europe'. He cites the German Catholic historian Joseph Lortz:

> It was a direct attack on the traditional sacramental concept, that is, against the objectivity of the divine life operative in the Church's liturgy. Here the resolution of Christianity into a religion of inner feeling was achieved at the very point at which its victory would have its greatest impact. Here was assailed the secret centre of the Church's unity ... For the Catholic Church it was not the attack on the Papacy that was the most fateful event which happened in the Reformation, but the emptying out from her Mysteries of the objective source of power'.[7]

Yet this 'emptying out' of the 'objectivity of the divine life operative in the Church's liturgy' would not have happened, had Luther been content to receive the doctrine of divine revelation through the instrumental mediation of the Church, which is to say the visible community convened by Christ. That was Trent's point in first affirming the Church as the repository of revelation. It was on that basis that Trent developed its doctrine of sacramental and liturgical life, and its doctrine of human participation in the work of the redemption. At the core of that doctrine we find the affirmation of the Mass as a 'true sacrifice . . . propitiatory for the living and the dead'.

Luther's objection to the traditional doctrine of the sacrifice of the Mass was that it was a 'work'; something which belonged to the instrumental mediation of the Church and to the active participation of humanity in the redemption. In Dr Clark's account of the matter, he 'arrived at a theology in which there was no place for any created reality to mediate to men God's salutary action, nor for any active sharing by men in the dispensation of grace'.[8] Hence:

> This fundamental difference which divides the Catholic conception of God's dealings with men from the Protestant may be described as a theology of *mediation* and *participation*. In Catholic thought, Christ's manhood, and the Church which is its fullness, and the sacraments which are his actions, form a hierarchy of created means by which the God-man communicates to men his saving activity. There is therefore a 'descending' and 'ascending' mediation: through a channel of created causes God reaches down to men, as it were, to bring them his salvation, and then implants in them a deiform principle, sanctifying grace, which begins and energizes their ascent towards ultimate union with himself.[9]

In this economy of instrumental mediation and participation in the saving work of Christ the eucharistic sacrifice holds the central place. Here the sacrifice of the cross is made available

> for all men in succeeding ages. In this great 'work' mortal priests are the vicars and instruments of the immortal High Priest. 'Thus does the particular doctrine of the Eucharistic sacrifice grow out of the general truth of the Mediation of

Christ', observed R. I. Wilberforce, the Tractarian divine; 'it is nothing more than the admission of this truth, taken in connection with the fact of the Real Presence'. With his customary discernment, Wilberforce pointed out that Luther's rejection of the sacrifice was bound up with his doctrine of justification.[10]

Conversely, the Tridentine doctrine of justification finds its supreme expression in the Council's teaching that the sacrifice of Christ sacramentally mediated, involves a real participation of the faithful who, 'with upright heart and true faith' elicit at Mass, in Christ, and with him, a return of mercy and grace for the living and the dead. The doctrine of intercession is inseparable from the doctrine of the eucharist proclaimed at Trent. Because Christ is 'truly, really and substantially present' in the eucharist, by *conversio* which 'the Catholic Church calls transubstantiation',[11] so is he truly, really and substantially present in his members. Hence the actions of redeemed humanity are endowed with a meritorious capacity, and a potentiality for intercession which are the fruit of Christ's merits actualized in the faithful members of his body the Church. Here the anthropology of the enslaved will is put to rest.[12]

Precisely because Christ is present in his members, so can they intercede with him and be heard. The Tridentine Profession of Faith therefore declares, in favour of the faithful still experiencing purification of heart, that the souls detained in purgatory 'are helped by the acts of intercession (*suffragiis*) of the faithful; likewise that the saints reigning together with Christ should be venerated and invoked, that they offer prayers to God for us, and that their relics should be venerated' (for these are sacramentals, aids to grace). Equally, 'the power of indulgences has been left by Christ to the Church' (for these are but a particular instance of the Church's dispensation of grace).

Interior regeneration, and the participation of the faithful in the work of the redemption; intercession, merit and the forgiveness of sins: these are the hallmarks of the sacramental understanding of salvation which we find in the decrees of Trent, and in the Profession of Faith which encapsulates its teaching. It adds up to a doctrine of the human person reconstituted in communion with the very life of God; a communion of grace and of will; a communion of sanctification; a communion whereby God so completely delivers himself to his members that they are empowered to depend upon him in each other, thereby honouring the work of his redemption from within humanity itself. Supremely is this true of the honour due to the Mother of God, whom the Council declares to be exempt from original sin by a special privilege of God. Inwardly to appreciate this doctrine is to arrive at a true evaluation of the fullness and the implications of redemption. In the person of Mary we see the action of the redeemer completely received and transmitted.

The Tridentine Profession of Faith concludes with an acknowledgement of the 'holy, catholic and apostolic, Roman Church as the mother and teacher of all Churches'. From this there followed a duty of obedience to the Roman Pontiff as the successor to St Peter, and the renunciation of all heresies condemned by the Church. Those who made the Profession of Faith undertook to do all in their power to see that it be received by those for whom they had the responsibility of cure of souls.

For four centuries the Profession of Faith was made by all beneficed priests with cure of souls, by all who professed Theology, Philosophy or Canon Law in the Church's seminaries or institutes of learning, and by all who entered the Catholic Church as converts. In 1877 it was extended to include the teaching of the First Vatican Council, and in particular, its teaching about papal primacy and infallibility. In 1910 Pius X added the Anti-Modernist Oath. There matters stood until the Second Vatican Council (1962-65). After the Council, in 1967, a new Profession of Faith was issued, to replace the Tridentine Profession, requiring subscription to the Nicene Creed and to 'each and all things pertaining to the doctrine of faith and morals' taught by the Church, and particularly to what pertains to 'the mystery of Christ's Holy Church, her Sacraments and Sacrifice of the Mass and the Primacy of the Roman Pontiff'.[13]

The essential perspective uniting the Second Vatican Council with the Council of Trent is its doctrine concerning the dignity of the human person, and the ground of that dignity. But what of the reception of Trent's teaching in historical actuality? Here we must take due account of the impediments in the religious culture and psychology of the sixteenth and succeeding centuries.

More and Erasmus were not alone in remarking upon the Manichaean image of God and man discernible in the outlook of the early Protestant reformers. Trent remarked on the phenomenon.[14] So too did the bishop of Verona, Gian Matteo Giberti in 1542. Commenting on the flight from Italy of the Capuchin preacher, Bernardino Ochino, Giberti found the probable explanation in Ochino's pessimism about the Church, and his pessimism about the Redeemer:

> either his zeal concerning the bad government ('mal governo') which he discerned in the Church, and this did not begin today and was from the beginning and there will always be good and bad . . . the other thing may have been the unease he had about the severity of our Saviour.[15]

In reality, both were linked. Giberti's analysis went to the root of the matter. If late mediaeval and renaissance Europe bred a Manichaeism distrustful of the 'benign nature' of almighty God, and uneasy about the 'severity' of the Redeemer, the responsibility lay in large measure with the images of paternal indifference projected by her pastors. Paul III's commission of reform traced the evils of the Church to their root in the practice of simony. Cardinal Pole, at the Council of Trent, extended the analysis to the whole of Christendom's pastoral leadership, ecclesiastical and civil. In the failure of pastoral care, he found the explanation for the divisions of Church and civil society.[16] Pole's call for a Church of penitence provides the correct perspective from which to assess the question of the reception of the doctrine of Trent; a question which turns on the Church's fidelity to the Holy Spirit, and in particular to the Tridentine legislation on pastoral and spiritual renewal. Were we to reflect on the anthropology of Jansenism, or the arid quibbles of the 'quarrel of grace' which mark the theological world of seventeenth century Catholicism, we might incline to the view that the reception of the Tridentine heritage was significantly impeded from within, and that the anthropological revolution of the Enlightment therefore found the Church insufficiently responsive in its theology of the redemption.

Yet such a verdict would need to be tempered by a consideration of the real pastoral achievements of the Catholic Reformation, and also by an exploration of the contemplative tradition of theology. In the spirituality of the Ignatian *Exercises*, in the *Works* of St John of the Cross, and in the writings of St Francis de Sales, we find lucid expression of the living doctrine of the emancipation and conversion of the will by the action of divine love. In particular, the *Treatise on the Love of God* by St Francis de Sales (1616), so majestically traces the course of human response to the divine initiative, a response which can be summed up in the word election, as to constitute the classic account, from within the Tridentine world, of the issues of grace and religious psychology precipitated by the Reformation.[17] It is this tradition of contemplative writing, of theology issuing from prayer, which, sustained and developed in theologians such as Möhler, Newman and Marmion, is likeliest to engage the ecumenical enterprise at its most promising angle of convergence: a convergence which arises from the action of the Holy Spirit, theologically discerned. Within the Protestant world, we can see already in the seventeenth century, a movement in favour of dissolving the rigid dichotomies of grace and the enslaved will; while within the evangelical world of the nineteenth and twentieth centuries we find renewed sensitivity to the primacy of charity arising from Divine Love. Probably the most pressing ecumenical need of the present hour is to integrate these movements within a renewed theology of grace and human freedom; a theology which will do full justice to the reality of original sin and the redemption.[13]

---

[1] *A Dialogue Concerning Heresies*, ed. W. E. Campbell under the title *The Dialogue Concerning Tyndale by Sir Thomas More*, (London [1927]), Bk. 4, ch. 12, p. 299. For Möhler's later development of the anthropological critique, cf. F. Heyer, *The Catholic Church from 1648 to 1870*, trans. W. D. Shaw (London [1969]), pp. 127ff.

[2] The Profession of Faith is published in H. Denzinger and A Schönmetzer, S.J., ed., *Enchiridion Symbolorum Definitionum et Declarationum de Rebus Fidei et Morum* (36th edition, Freiburg im Breisgau [1965]), pp. 425-427. An English text in J. Neuner, S.J., and J. Dupuis, S.J., ed., *The Christian Faith in the Doctrinal Documents of the Catholic Church* (2nd edn., Dublin and Cork [1976]), pp. 21-24. The definitive edition of the General Councils of the Church may be found in G. Alberigo *et. al.*, ed., *Conciliorum Oecumenicorum Decreta* (3rd edn., Bologna [1973]). For the circumstances surrounding the publication of the Profession of Faith, cf. 'Pie IV', by G. Constant in *Dictionnaire de Théologie Catholique*, vol. 12, cols. 1640-41, and J. Broderick, S.J., *Saint*

Peter Canisius (London [1935]), p. 609.

[3] Alberigo, p. 684; Neuner and Dupuis, p. 351. Council of Trent, Decree on the Sacraments (1547).

[4] A point emphasized by John A. Hardon, S.J. *The Catholic Catechism* (New York [1974]), p. 183, citing the Tridentine Decree on Justification, 7 (Alberigo, p. 673). Hardon's *Catechism* provides an excellent doctrinal account of the issues examined in this essay.

[5] I am grateful to Fr Francis Selman for drawing my attention to Augustine's teaching on this point in *De spiritu et littera* 52: 'From freedom comes love (dilectio).' Cf. also J. N. D. Kelly *Early Christian Doctrines* (5th edn., London [1977]), p. 368.

[6] Quoted by Francis Clark, S.J., *Eucharistic Sacrifice and the Reformation* (2nd [1967] impression with corrections, reprinted Devon, [1981]), p. 107.

[7] Quoted by Clark, *Eucharistic Sacrifice*, *loc. cit.*

[8] *Eucharistic Sacrifice*, p. 106.

[9] *Ibid.*, p. 105.

[10] *Ibid.*, p. 106.

[11] Professor Chadwick remarks on the 'paradox in the embarrassment evident at Trent in the treatment of "imputation"' since the Mass and the doctrine of eucharistic sacrifice is 'in essential principle a proclamation of imputed righteousness'. ('Justification by Faith: a Perspective', in *One in Christ*, [1984-3], pp. 191-225, at pp. 221-2). But this depends on reinstating Luther's account of the matter (above, p. 49) while ignoring the text of what Trent itself has to say about the doctrine of eucharistic sacrifice. The 'paradox' dissolves once we employ Clark's 'theological key' (above, p. 49): viz., the essential connection between the Mass and the doctrine of justification.

[12] Neuner and Dupuis, *The Christian Faith*, p. 23.

[13] *Acta Apostolicae Sedis* (Vatican City, vol. 59, [1967]), p. 1058. Cf. also the *Profession of Faith of Paul VI* (1968) in Neuner and Dupuis, pp. 24-31.

[14] Hardon, *The Catholic Catechism*, p. 75, citing the Tridentine canons on justification, 6 (Alberigo, p. 679).

[15] A. Prosperi, *Tra Evangelismo e Controriforma : G. M. Giberti* (Rome [1969]), cited by A. D. Wright, 'L'Eglise ou la Foi: la rupture en Italie' in *Les Réformes: Enracinement Socio-Culturel. XXVe colloque international d'études humanistes, Tours, 1er-13 juillet 1982*, ed. B. Chevalier et Robert Sauzet, p. 383.

[16] Pole's remarks on the avarice and ambition of Christian leaders as the root cause of the maladies of Christendom's afflictions were proffered by way of an examination of conscience to the fathers of the Council. Cf. D. Fenlon, *Heresy and Obedience in Tridentine Italy: Cardinal Pole and the Counter Reformation* (Cambridge [1972]), p. 119.

[17] Election, as understood by St Francis de Sales, means a preferential love given

to God. The word he uses is Augustine's word, and Trent's word, *dilectio*. Thus on the question of how human works are meritoriously related to God's works, he writes of the 'Holy Spirit who, "dwelling in our hearts by charity" (Rom 5⁵) does these works in us, for us, and with us with such exquisite art that these very works which are wholly ours are still more wholly his.' (Book 11, ch. 6, p. 211, trans. John K. Ryan, 2 vols, Illinois [1974], vol. 2). The *Treatise* deserves to be taken as a central text in ecumenical discussion.

[18] 'The inability to understand "original sin" and to make it understandable' in a culture dominated by the assumption that man is good by nature, and corrupted only by false education and social structure, is at the heart of the contemporary failure to understand the necessity of Christ the Redeemer, in the view of Joseph, Cardinal Ratzinger. *The Ratzinger Report*, ed., V. Messori (San Francisco [1986]), p. 79.

The Thirty-nine Articles

C. W. Dugmore, D.D., Emeritus Professor of Ecclesiastical
History,
University of London

From 1521 onwards every ruler, government and people in
Western Europe had to face and answer three fundamental
questions: (1) Do you accept the authority of the papacy as the
Head of the Church of Christ in all matters of faith and morals?
If not, what authority will you substitute for it? (2) Do you
accept the doctrines, creed and ritual of the Roman Church as
true and binding on all Christians? If not, what doctrine and
ritual are binding, and by what authority are they to be declared
and enforced? (3) What is the relation of the State, i.e. the
secular power, to the Church, i.e. the spiritual power?

In Germany the *Confession of Augsburg* [1530] soon became
the chief standard of faith in the Lutheran churches and, as we
shall see, had some influence ultimately on the English *Thirty-
nine Articles*. In England there appeared in 1536 the *Ten Articles*.
'deuised by the Kynges highnes maiestie, to stablyshe christen
quietnes and unitie amonge us, and to avoyde contentious
opinions, which articles be also approved by the consent and
determination of the hole clergie of this realme', according to
the version printed by Thomas Berthelet, the King's printer.[1]
Briefly the *Ten* were divided into five which dealt with 'The
Principal Articles concerning our faith' which were declared to
'be comprehended in the whole body and canon of the Bible,
and also in the three Creeds', namely, the sacraments of

baptism, penance and 'of the Altar', and justification: the last five concerned the 'laudable ceremonies used in the Church'. Hot on the heels of the *Ten Articles* came the first Royal Injunctions of Henry VIII [1536], which required the clergy not only to keep the laws abolishing the jurisdiction of the Pope in England and establishing the authority of the King as Supreme Head of *Ecclesia Anglicana*, but also ordering them to expound the Articles regularly to their flocks and to 'provide a book of the whole Bible, both in Latin, and also in English , and lay the same in the choir, for every man that will to look and read thereon, and shall discourage no man from the reading of any part of the Bible . . . but rather comfort, exhort and admonish every man to read the same as the very word of God, and the spiritual food of man's soul'.[2] Thus the doctrinal basis of the Church of England was clearly to be the Bible and the creeds of the first four General Councils of the church, And the authority by which this was to be enacted? The King and the 'hole clergie of this realme' in Convocation. Later parliament also came into the picture by passing various statutes, culminating in 'The Subscription (Thirty-nine Articles) Act' of 1571 (13 Eliz. cap. 12).

The background to the Thirty-nine Articles is somewhat complicated. In the course of the attempt by Henry VIII to secure from Pope Leo X a declaration that his marriage to Catherine of Aragon was null and void, despite the fact that he had written a treatise against Luther which had won him the title 'Defender of the Faith', Henry decided to enter into negotiations with the German Lutheran princes in order to 'twist the Pope's elbow'. In 1538 a group of Lutheran divines from Germany were invited to England by Henry to confer with a committee of English divines to draw up, if possible, a joint Confession of Faith. In a bundle of Archbishop Cranmer's papers preserved in the State Paper Office (now the Public Record Office) Henry Jenkyns discovered a draft of the 'Thirteen Articles' agreed on between the English and German divines, which were never published nor in any way imposed upon the English Church. As Jenkyns remarked, there is a strong resemblance in them to the *Confession of Augsburg*.[3] The 'Thirteen Articles' covered the following subjects: 'Of the unity of of God and the Trinity of Persons'; 'Of Original Sin'; 'Of the Two Natures of Christ'; 'Of Justification'; 'Of the Church'; 'Of Baptism'; 'Of the Eucharist'; 'Of Penance'; 'Of the use of the Sacraments'; 'Of the Ministers of the Church'; 'Of the Rites of the Church'; 'Of Civil Affairs'; 'Of the Resurrection of Bodies and the Last Judgment'. 'Of these the first three are taken almost word for word from the Confession of Augsburg', observed E. C. S. Gibson, 'the influence which may be traced in other parts of the Articles as well'.[4] But although Cranmer incorporated, for example, most of the Lutheran article 'On Original Sin', he made some significant changes and additions to the wording of the corresponding Augsburg article. Instead of defining the state of fallen men as 'born with sin, that is, without the fear of God etc.', he wrote 'born with original sin, that is with deprivation of the original righteousness which ought to inhere, whence they are sons of wrath and are deficient in the understanding of God, the fear of God etc. . . . And they have concupiscence, repugnant to the law of God, whence is an original disease or flaw'. Thus Cranmer avoided the Lutheran and Calvinist insistence on 'total depravity' and bequeathed to the Church of England the traditional teaching adopted at the council of Trent in 1546 that Adam and his successors lost the original righteousness in which had been constituted, incurred the divine anger and have been changed for the worse (*in deterius commutatum fuisse*).

The 'Thirteen Articles', after revision, formed the basis of the Edwardian 'Forty-two Articles' submitted to the Privy Council in May 1552 and issued on 12 June, 1553 by royal mandate to the officials of the province of Canterbury, requiring subscription from all clergy, schoolmasters, and members of the universities of Oxford and Cambridge on admission to degrees.[5] This was the first occasion on which subscription to a set of articles was required in the Church of England.

Much has been written about the title of the 'Forty-two Articles',[6] as set out in the English edition published by Grafton, viz. 'Articles agreed on by the bishops and other learned men in the Synod at London'; similarly in the Latin edition printed by Wolfe; and, more specifically, 'in the last convocation at London' in the edition by Day (all dated 1553). 'This is untrue', says Constant categorically. 'Cranmer complained about the title page to Warwick and the Council but no notice was taken of his complaint. The new creed was imposed upon the nation solely by the will of a King who was a minor and of the Government'.[7] Already in the late seventeenth century Gilbert Burnet had written 'it appears by a variety of evidences that these Articles were not passed in convocation, nor so much as offered to it'.[8]

It is obvious from their contents that these Articles were never intended to provide a complete system of theology. Indeed, the title prefixed to the first English edition of Grafton stated that they were agreed upon 'for the avoiding of controversy in opinions, and the establishment of a godly concord in certain matters of religion'. Thus, while Article I ('Of Faith in the Holy Trinity') expresses general belief in the unity of God in three Persons, there is nothing here or in Article II ('The Word of God made very man') about the divinity of Christ or his eternal relation to the Father. There is no article on the

Holy Spirit and, while the sufficiency of Scripture for salvation is asserted in Article V, there is nothing about the Canon of Holy Scripture nor any list of the canonical books. Again, nothing is said of Confirmation or of Penance. The Articles were designed to refute the errors of Rome, on the one hand, and the Anabaptists, on the other. Thus Roman or mediaeval errors were condemned in Article XII (the teaching of the 'school authors' on congruous merit), XIII (Works of supererogation), XXIII ('The doctrine of school-authors concerning purgatory, pardons, worshipping and adoration, as well of images as of relics, and also invocation of saints, is a fond thing vainly feigned, and grounded upon no warrant of Scripture, but rather repugnant to the word of God'); XXIX (transubstantiation) and XXX ('the sacrifices of masses').

Although the Anabaptists are only mentioned by name in two of the Articles – VIII (Of original sin) and XXXVII (Christian men's goods are not common), Hardwick and Gibson both pointed out long ago that the attack on Anabaptism can be seen in eighteen or more of these Articles.

Edward VI died less than a month after the issuing of the 'Forty-two Articles'. They had not been authorized by Statute and so there was no Act of Parliament to be repealed under the Catholic Queen Mary. They were quietly forgotten during her reign.

By the end of the first year of Elizabeth I the so-called Settlement of Religion had been achieved by the passing of the Act of Supremacy [April 1559] and of Uniformity (immediately afterwards), the latter ordering the use of Edward VI's Second Prayer Book [1552] with certain alterations and additions and no other book, under severe penalties, from 24 June. Elizabeth's Royal Injunctions followed.[9] All of these documents contained statements about the doctrine and practice of the Church, but none of them provided doctrinal definitions. Even the Prayer Books only contained the three catholic Creeds and a short children's catechism.

'The Convocation of 1563 prepared the Articles of Religion, that doctrinal statement which remains four centuries later a classic, if anachronistic, expression of the Anglican understanding of the Christian Faith.'[10] However, before we can discuss the proceedings of that Convocation, we must consider one or two other attempts to define the doctrines of the Church of England between the Forty-two Articles of 1553 and the Articles agreed in 1563.

In the Convocation of February 1559 the Marian clergy approved a set of five articles which asserted that in the sacrament of the altar there is present really (*realiter*) the natural body of Christ born of the Virgin Mary and likewise his natural blood; that after consecration there remains no substance of bread and wine but only the substance of God and Man; the propitiatory sacrifice of the true body of Christ in the Mass; the supreme power of 'feeding and ruling' the church on earth enjoyed by Peter and his successors in the apostolic see; and that authority to define things concerning faith, sacraments and discipline belong to the clergy and not to the laity.[11] But the Act of Supremacy required all bishops and clergy and all temporal officers of the Crown to take an oath on the Gospel affirming the royal supremacy and repudiating all foreign jurisdictions and authorities. The only one of the sixteen bishops who took the oath was Kitchen, Bishop of Llandaff; all the rest refused and were deprived during the course of the year. So the ranks of the episcopate were filled by non-papists, like Matthew Parker, who became Archbishop of Canterbury. Richard Cox, who had been the leader of the English congregation in exile in Frankfurt during Mary's reign and who now became Bishop of Ely, Edmund Grindal (London), Edwin Sandys (Winchester), and so on. Were they and some of their like-minded clergy 'Anglicans'? Not, I think, in any sense which would be meaningful today. They were Protestants who supported the Elizabethan Settlement, the traditional organization of the Church in England through a threefold ministry, divided into provinces dioceses and parishes, the ecclesiastical courts, and the Book of Common Prayer annexed to the 1559 Act of Uniformity. The Puritans were godly, pious radicals who were not satisfied with the Settlement, and wanted to get rid of anything remotely connected with popery and carry reform of the church much further than it had gone already. It is probably best to describe the two groups as 'Puritan' and 'non-Puritan', since it is really unhistorical to speak of 'Anglicans' and 'Anglicanism' before 1593, the year in which Richard Hooker published his great work *Of the Laws of Ecclesiastical Polity* and Parliament passed an Act against Seditious Sectaries. Both groups were Protestant and both supported the Royal Supremacy.

These, then, were the men who met in the Convocation of 1563 and set in motion the Thirty-nine Articles. As early as 1559 a number of returned Marian emigrés had prepared a 'Declaration of Doctrine' for the Queen.[12] 'It is professedly based on the Forty-two, the Edwardian Articles, which it recapitulates and occasionally expands or interprets'.[13] Next, 'A declaration of certain principal articles of religion set out by order of both archbishops and metropolitans, and the rest of the bishops for the uniformity of doctrine, to be taught and holden of all parsons, vicars and curates . . . as necessary for the instruction of their people; to be read . . . at their possession-taking, or first entry into their cures, and also after that, yearly at two several times . . . immediately after the gospel'[14] was required by item 29 of the 'Interpretations of the Bishops'[15] and item 3 of the Lambeth Articles of 12 April, 1561[16] 'to be used throughout the realm uniformly'. Neither the Queen, Parliament, nor Convocation sanctioned them, so that they rested solely on the authority of the bishops.

In the Convocation of 1563 a thorough revision and expansion of the Forty-two Articles was undertaken. Four new Articles were added, namely Article V 'Of the Holy Ghost', Article XII 'Of Good Works', Article XXIX 'Of the wicked who do not eat the Body of Christ in the use of the Lord's Supper', and Article XXX 'Of both kinds'. Article XXIX had been prepared by Parker in his draft before the meeting of Convocation and it is in his manuscript copy at Corpus Christi College, Cambridge, with the signatures of the bishops who subscribed to it on 29 January, but it was omitted from the printed version of the Thirty-eight Articles of 1563 published by authority of the Queen and it may be that its omission was due to 'the direct intervention of the Queen herself'.[17] It was restored in the final version by the Convocation of 1571, thus making up the number to Thirty-nine again.

In Article II 'Of the Word or Son of God' which, as we noted earlier,[18] in the 1553 Article contained nothing about the divinity of Christ or his relation to the Father, a new phrase was inserted: 'begotten from everlasting of the Father, the very and eternal God, of one substance with the Father'. Article VI (= V of 1553) defines the Canonical Books of the Old and New Testaments 'of whose authority was never any doubt in the Church' and lists them, at the same time listing the books of the Apocrypha, which 'the Church doth read for example of life and instruction of manners, but yet doth it not apply them to establish any doctrine'. Article VIII (= VII of 1553) on the three

Creeds adds 'and believed' after the words 'ought thoroughly to be received'. There are other similar minor verbal additions. But, more important, is the omission of the 1553 Article X 'Of grace' together with the re-writing of the present Article X (= IX of 1553) 'Of Free-Will' and XI 'Of the Justification of Man'. In Article XVII 'Of Predestination and Election' the phrase 'though the decrees of predestination are unknown to us' in the last paragraph is omitted before the words 'we must receive God's promises in such wise as they be generally set forth to us in Holy Scripture'.

The most important changes concern the Eucharist, which alongside Justification and Predestination, formed one of the two main areas of dispute among all the Reformers. Article XXV (= XXVI of 1553) 'Of the Sacraments' was re-written (i) to differentiate between the two 'sacraments ordained of Christ' and 'those five commonly called sacraments' (this was new) and (ii) to get rid of the explicit condemnation of the phrase *ex opere operato*. Article XXVIII 'Of the Lord's Supper' omits altogether the third clause of the corresponding 1553 Article (XXIX) which stated that the faithful should not believe in 'the real and bodily presence', on the ground that a man's body cannot be present in many places at once and, anyhow, Christ's body is in heaven; substitutes 'partaking' for 'communion' (of the body and blood of Christ); and adds the important positive statement that 'the body of Christ is given, taken, and eaten, in the Supper, only after an heavenly and spiritual manner. And the mean whereby the Body of Christ is received and eaten in the Supper is Faith'. The plain meaning of this is that the Presence is there (spiritually, not bodily) independent of us, and is thus offered to all, but that the faithful only are able receive it. The change in Article XXVIII involving the omission of the clause denying the real presence was doubtless distasteful to the Puritans, as were many other things in the Elizabethan Articles, such as the addition to Article XX that 'The Church hath power to decree rites or ceremonies and authority in controversies of faith', and that in Article XXXVII 'Where we attribute to the Queen's majesty the chief government . . . they [the Princes] should . . . restrain with the civil sword the stubborn and evildoers'.

The Articles were passed by Convocation and authorization by the Queen in their Latin version. Eight years later the Thirty-eight Articles of 1563 were reconsidered by Convocation and all Thirty-nine were now approved by the Queen since her excommunication the previous year had removed the need to avoid giving offence to the papists. Thus, in 1571, Parliament came into the picture and with the Queen's assent passed an 'Act to reform certain disorders touching Ministers of the Church', generally known as The Subscription (Thirty-nine Articles) Act, 1571 (13 Eliz. cap. 12)[19] This enacted that 'no person shall hereafter be admitted to any benefice with cure except he . . . shall first have subscribed the said Articles in presence of the ordinary, and publicly read the same in the parish church of that benefice, with declaration of his unfeigned assent to the same'. Subscription was required only from the clergy and never from the laity, except in the case of persons supplicating for degrees in the universities of Oxford and Cambridge, and this requirement was finally abolished by the Universities Test Act of 1871 (34 Vict. cap. 26). Meanwhile, the Clerical Subscription Act of 1865 (28 and 29 Vict. cap. 1232) substituted for subscriptions a 'Declaration of Assent': 'I assent to the Thirty-nine Articles of Religion and to the Book of Common Prayer . . . I believe the doctrine . . . as therein set forth, to be agreeable to the Word of God.' This Declaration is still made by all clergy on induction to a benefice.

Despite the stricture of Professor A. G. Dickens[20] that 'the Anglican Church has been left with a rather heavy clutter of anachronisms. . . . At least we are no longer terrified by Anabaptism! . . . However strongly one may reject the Articles as a statement of twentieth-century thinking in the Anglican Church . . . however much they may now savour of long-dead ecclesiastical politics . . . they still deserve serious study as a historical monument, and even as a point of departure for any new codes which may be attempted'. In view of the virtual demise of the Book of Common Prayer it is valuable that there still exists one link with the reformed Ecclesia Anglicana, both Catholic and Protestant, which emerged in the sixteenth century.

[1] Reprinted in *English Historical Documents 1485-1558*, ed. C. H. Williams (London [1967]), 795-805.

[2] *Ibid.*, 805-808.

[3] *Remains of Thomas Cranmer*, ed. H. Jenkyns (Oxford [1883]), iv. 273, cf. i. xxii-xxiv; C. Hardwick, *A History of the Articles of Religion* (Cambridge [1859]), 60-61.

[4] Edgar C. S. Gibson, *The Thirty-nine Articles of the Church of England* (2nd edn., London [1898]), 7.

[5] Gibson, *op. cit.*, 14.

[6] They are printed in Hardwick, *op. cit.*, Appendix iii; G. Burnet, *The History of the Reformation*, ed. N. Pocock (Oxford [1865]), v. 314-329; *Liturgies of King Edward VI* (Parker Society, Cambridge [1844]), 526-537.

[7] G. Constant, *The Reformation in England*, trans. E. I. Watkin (London [1941]), ii. 298; cf. W. K. Jordan, *Edward VI: The Threshold of Power* (London [1970]), 355.

[8] Burnet, *op. cit.*, iii. 373.

[9] They are printed in *Visitation Articles and Injunctions of the Period of the Reformation* (Alcuin Club Collections xvi, ed. W. H. Frere, London [1910]), iii. 8-29, and in *Select Statutes and Other Constitutional Documents etc.*, ed. G. W. Prothero (Oxford, 3rd edn. [1906]), 184-190.

[10] William P. Haugaard, *Elizabeth and the English Reformation* (Cambridge [1968]), 247.

[11] E. Cardwell, *Synodalia* (Oxford [1842]), ii. 492-493.

[12] This very wordy document is contained in Corpus Christi College, Cambridge, MS. cxxi 20, which has not been printed, though R. W. Dixon, *History of the Church of England* (Oxford [1902]), v. 107 ff. gives an account of its contents. Strype (*Annals*, i, pt i. 167-172) refers to it and prints in full the long introduction and conclusion.

[13] Dixon, *loc. cit.*

[14] Printed in E. Cardwell, *Documentary Annals* (Oxford [1844]), i. 263-267.

[15] Frere, *op. cit.*, iii. 72.

[16] *ibid.*, 95.

[17] E. C. S. Gibson, *The Thirty-Nine Articles*, 668-669.

[18] See above, p. 165.

[19] H. Gee and W. J. Hardy, *Documents illustrative of English Church History,* 477-480.

[20] *The English Reformation,* 252-253.

The Westminster Confession of Faith

PROFESSOR J. K. S. REID, C.B.E., T.D., M.A., D.D.,
EDINBURGH

1. Confession

THE Reformation reactivated an inclination to compile statements of faith that had long been dormant in the church. To this credal resurgence the Westminster Confession of Faith belongs as late-comer. The reasons and motives behind this theological activity were many, various, and not particularly obscure. In essence they were not different from those that operated in NT and post-apostolic times; but there are altered emphases. The Christian church at the beginning made its confession in two words: *kyrios Christos* Jesus is Lord (1 Jn 4[2f], Rom 10[9], esp. NEB). This confession included the elements of *praise* (of God, doxological), *proclamation* (of the truth, theological), and practice (renunciation of Caesar as Lord, with the civil penalties incurred, see Rev 13[15-17], praxilogical). The documents of the Reformation in the four decades following Luther's 95 Theses are much longer than the two words of NT confession, or even the circumlocutions of the Athanasian Creed. But the same notes are discernible in all: *joy* at the recovery of the gospel, whose essential *truth* is salvation by grace alone, setting us free for *works* of grateful service for the glory of God and benefit of man.

2. Theological development

From the beginning the theological element is involved in

development, and thus are incurred the dangers against which Augustine warned when he said: *fides terminatur non in imaginem sed in rem*. The one-membered baptismal formula of the NT develops into a three-membered trinitarian confession (see Oscar Cullman: *The Earliest Christian Confessions* [1949]). Irenaeus, the Niceno-Constantinopolitan Creed, and the evolution of the Apostles' Creed show a similar tendency. Christianity is impelled to such development largely to respond positively to a demand for elucidation of what the Christian faith is and implies, and negatively to retort to those, whether inside or outside the church, who advance doctrines destructive of the gospel. When a 'reason' is asked (1 Pet 3[15]) the church has to reply – as Augustine says, *ne taceretur*; when the gospel is attacked or traduced, a corrective statement has to be issued – again as Augustine, *non sponte sed coactu*. Inevitably such action has an exclusive consequence: a line of distinction is drawn marking off those unable or unwilling to accept the statement.

3. *The Reformation*

The Reformation gave rise to similar demands and responses, and the extended credal statements of the period manifest the three basic elements of confession. But the theological element rises to a dominance in which praise and practice are subdued or even stifled. No one in his senses would try to sing the Augustana, let alone the WCF. Reformed church people will obviously not buy indulgences, but it is not possible to trace back differences in conduct between Lutherans and Calvinists to their different views of the Eucharist. But the situation cried out for proclamation. Both Christendom and the world at large were entitled to know how Reformed churches interpreted the gospel. So the Scots Confession 1560 'notified to the world the sum of that doctrine which we profess'.

4. *The Westminster Confession of Faith*

In the Scots Confession the Reformed Church in Scotland made its point and declared its theological position. It takes an honoured place among the formularies of the first four decades of the Reformation. But three-quarters of a century after its acceptance by the Scottish Church, renewed incentive to credal definition arose from a quite other source and in quite different circumstances. The Parliament at Westminster appointed a synod (1643-49) to 'reform the English Church'. Among its completed business this Westminster Assembly, with considerable help from a tiny and temporary representation from Scotland, drew up the Westminster Confession of Faith, 'as part of the covenanted uniformity of religion betwixt the Churches of Christ in the Kingdoms of Scotland, England and Ireland'. Repudiated, or perhaps more exactly disregarded, by almost all sections of the church in England, this Confession was 'approved' by the Scottish General Assembly 1647, and 'ratified and established' by the Scottish Parliament 1649. Here is a web of anomalies indeed. Issued not by a church court but by a parliament-appointed commission,[1] written by 151 representatives of the 'English Church' plus only eight from Scotland, designed to promote a national 'uniformity' that was never achieved – this is the document that becomes 'the public and avowed Confession' of the church in Scotland, and is designated from perhaps 1851 as the 'subordinate standard' in the determination of its faith and life; and, in no sense a Presbyterian creation, it comes to be generally used throughout the Presbyterian world.

5. *A changed theological climate*

It was entirely proper that a newly reformed church should make its own restatement of the faith. But since the Scots Confession had been formulated, many changes had taken place that were not propitious to a satisfactory discharge of the task.

(*a*) Early on it is the unreformed Church of Rome from which distinction had to be chiefly made. At first the distinction is drawn in conciliatory terms. The Augustana (1530) was designed to show that 'Lutherans departed in no vital and essential respect from the Catholic Church, or even the Roman Church, as revealed in its earlier writers' (W. Walker: *A History of the Christian Church* [1932], 372). But now the Council of Trent had come and gone. Rome had had its chance to edge towards some reformation of itself, and the chance had not been taken. The Church of Rome could thus only be regarded as irreconcilable. Hence references to it lose their conciliatory tone and become combative. The Church of Rome ranks with the 'synagogues of satan', and the Pope is 'that antichrist' (WCF 25.5,6).

(*b*) The Reformation itself was fissured by divisions, as its churches engaged in controversy among themselves. Hence the credal statements formulated come to stake out areas the churches respectively occupy. Able no longer to command undivided Reformed acceptance, they become more sectarian in character. The attempt to find consensus between Lutheran and Reformed Churches collapses: they part, each going its own sweet way.

(*c*) A theological *rigor scholasticus* had settled upon the thought and spirit of the churches of the Reformation. A certain rationalistic conceit considered it possible and proper to pry into matters without practical or real importance and pronounce judgment on them. Those who so proceeded seem quite unaware that the more that is said in this vein the more vulnerable is it to disagreement, and the more rigidly imposed the more narrowly exclusive are the consequences.

(*d*) Concurrently or consequently, theological issues undreamt of in earlier times had arisen. A theological statement now had to take sides on matters trivial in importance compared with the great issues of the heyday of the Reformation. As sides were taken, what was said had the character less of a Christian manifesto than of a party broadcast: the trumpet call of the Reformation is replaced by the bickering of kettledrums, the *vexilla regis* by sectarian pennants.

6. *Character and content of WCF*

The first three chapters illustrate the greatness and the defectiveness of WCF, 'Of the Holy Scripture', 'Of God, and of the Holy Trinity', 'Of God's Eternal Decree'. Of all the Reformed confessional documents, only WCF gives scripture such formal priority. This priority is complemented by primacy in substantial importance: 'the whole counsel of God concerning all things necessary for his own glory, man's salvation, faith, and life, is either expressly set down in scripture, or by good and necessary consequence may be deduced from scripture' (1.6). The *sola Scriptura*, so often alleged as the paramount principle of Reformed churches, here receives classic expression. For the rest, the doctrine of Calvin is closely followed. But already an issue has arisen on which a contemporary statement has to take sides: what is the nature of biblical inspiration? Even in Calvin's day two main views were current, and Calvin has been variously interpreted as advocating each. WCF comes down unhesitatingly on one side: scripture is 'immediately inspired by God' (1.8, cf. 1.2 and 3).

Only in Chapter 2 does WCF come to the doctrine of God. Its expression reaches splendid heights, unexcelled in sonorous eloquence and even poetry. Yet the elaborate apparatus of biblical reference cannot conceal the fact that much use is made of the 'deduction' from scripture justified above, and that this deduction is in turn guided by or at least follows what others would with greater frankness call tradition, e.g. the unqualified acceptance of filioque (2.3). Nor indeed can the certain nominalism of 2.1, 2 be extracted from scripture without the historical maieutic intervention of a William of Occam.

The third chapter may claim to be the most celebrated and notorious, with its uncompromising statement of *praedestinatio duplex*. In its presentation of the 'awful' doctrine, WCF matches the calm majesty of Calvin's exposition. It is liberally equipped with biblical citations; yet scripture never uses 'decree' ('decrees' in Longer and Shorter catechisms) in this sense and connexion. The doctrine is really a 'deduction', not from scriptural evidence, but, with chilling logical symmetry, from a non-biblical use of the term. The theological consequences are disastrous: election precedes grace (as Calvin precisely says, *Inst*. 3.22.1); and the person and work of Christ are interpreted as merely instrumental in effecting a decision already made (see my *Concerning the Eternal Predestination of God* [1961], 40). Here too decision has to be taken about a matter of subsidiary importance but contemporary urgency: the issue between sub- and supra-lapsarians. Placing the eternal decree before even the creation, let alone the fall, forecloses the judgment of WCF in favour of the more forbidding alternative solution to a singularly arid and unreal issue.

Later on, as if belatedly to compensate for the icy remoteness of a divine counsel in which Christ has no part, WCF swings over to a marked interiorism: almost bypassing what

God has objectively done for us in Christ, it devotes nearly a third of its chapters to the benefits we derive therefrom, and the assurance thereby given of being among the elect.

7. Significance for its day

Despite its profoundly theological character, WCF was designed primarily as a constitutional document, and its compilation was determined by peremptory practical concerns. Ecclesiastical, religious, civil and political purposes were inextricably intertwined with theological interest. 'Uniformity of church government', 'unity in religion', 'peace in his Majesty's Dominions', 'a most firm and stable union between the two kingdoms of England and Scotland', opposition to 'all forms of tyranny', 'the utter extirpation of popery, prelacy, heresy, schism, superstition, and idolatry' – the influence of all these concerns, and also of changing fortunes on the battlefields of Naseby and Philiphaugh, is eminently discernible in the document that was to dominate theology in the Presbyterian family of churches.

The Westminster Assembly contrived with astonishing success to reconcile these interests, and at the same time to harmonize in one statement the varying theological emphases of episcopalian, independent, erastian, and presbyterian. The result is a clear and uncompromising statement of Calvinism in its scholastic phase, a crystallization of what came in Scotland to be called 'the second Reformation'.

The success proved to be in part short-lived and in part injurious. In England the ecclesiastical parties participant in the Assemble soon fell apart into a fragmentation that is still part of the English scene today. In contrast, Scotland and English-speaking Presbyterianisn took the work of the Assembly to its heart and too unreservedly into its life and thought. It was indeed a statement expressing with extraordinary exactness the mood and atmosphere of the day. More than in the case of any other Presbyterian Church, WCF comes to be interwoven into the theology and practice of the Church in Scotland. Here the flow of events after acceptance of WCF in 1638 continued. Fresh issues arose in the fifty years that followed. A 'Roman scare' developed, and also a 'fear of being swamped by "episcopal men"'. After the Revolution Settlement (1690), the Church of Scotland in 1694-1711 'devised legislation less for the "preservation of the faith" than for "the protection of the Presbyterian party into whose hands the Revolution had placed the ecclesiastical power in Scotland"' (James Cooper: *Confessions of Faith and Formulas of Subscription* [1907]). In similar mood the Church of Scotland in 1706-7 armoured itself against interference on the part of its other traditional adversary, the State: 'the true Protestant religion, as presently professed (is to) continue without any alteration in all succeeding generations'. Similarly, 'the Universities and colleges of St Andrews, Glasgow, Aberdeen, and Edinburgh, as now established by law, shall continue within this kingdom for ever'! The church is well on the way to becoming a mediaeval fortress instead of a pilgrim people of God.

8. *Use*

English-speaking Presbyterian churches have made WCF a cardinal element in the admission of office-bearers. The problem of how to exact adherence to a credal standard without violating the conscience and the proper freedom of the individual made its appearance as early as the beginning of the fourth century with the Nicene symbol; and it has agitated the Christian mind ever since. Scotland has had a particularly long and intimate acquaintance with the problem, and here and elsewhere a variety of solutions has been offered.

(a) At the outset, WCF was accepted in Scotland with certain 'reservation'.

(b) 'Interpretation' of the Confession is invoked and is specifically reserved to the church, and WCF is approved only 'as to the truth of the matter' – a significant qualifier.

(c) Distinctions come to be made: the Confession is approved only as 'containing the sum and substance of the doctrine of Reformed churches', and 'the grand mysteries and fundamental verities of the gospel' are distinguished from the Confession's 'determinations on matters of less importance.'

(d) For the last hundred years in Scotland, Declaratory Acts have played an important role, repeating the distinction between 'the great and fundamental truths and grand mysteries of the gospel' and 'unnecessary burdens as to forms of expression and matters which do not enter into the substance of the faith' (1870, United Free Church).

(e) This formulation becomes standard, and is today repeated at ordination of ministers and admission of elders. In the customary formula, WCF is referred to as 'subordinate standard' (though the phrase is only of 1851 provenance), and the church in exacting adherence to it is at the same time 'recognizing liberty of opinion on such points of doctrine as do not enter into the substance of the faith'. Of what constitutes 'agreement with the Word of God and the fundamental doctrines of the Christian faith contained in the said Confession . . . the church itself shall be sole judge'.

(f) Presbyterian churches in America have demanded acceptance of WCF by ministers 'as containing the system of doctrine taught in the Holy Scriptures'. Further, during the course of the present century they have adopted the device of revising the text of WCF. The chapter on marriage was re-written, and 'Of the Civil Magistrate' was considerably altered. A chapter was added 'Of the Holy Spirit' to remedy a grave and almost inexplicable omission. Another added chapter 'Of the Gospel' was designed to 'express the love of God for all men'. This illustrates how unsatisfactory or even impossible are attempts to revise a historical and historic document: 'all men' of the addition is irreconcilable with the uncompromising 'some men' of WCF 3.3 (cf. 8.8), and indeed 'the infinite and perfect love' of God with the Anselmic 'satisfied justice' of the God of 8.5.

(g) A more recent modification has frankly put WCF alongside other confessions of both earlier and later provenance, and accorded it a 'guiding' role, subordinate of course to scripture and also to ecumenical creeds. This line of action has been followed by Presbyterian churches in USA (in *The Worshipbook* [1972]), and also by the United Reformed Church in England (formed in 1972 by the Presbyterian and Congregational Churches).

9. Relevance today

The range of devices used to ease the strain WCF imposes on conscientious integrity is proof of grave dissatisfaction with the theology it contains and the role it has traditionally been allotted. Such qualifications and reservations upon strict adherence are emollients not remedies; and the credibility of WCF may well be thought to have 'died the death of a thousand qualifications'.

The perpetuation of a static relationship to this in many ways splendid theological statement, however modified, misconceives the role of theology in general and of confession in particular. The church has a continuing mandate to do theology. Trying faithfully to discharge it, the church keeps mobile and alert; neglecting it, the church slithers into stagnation and indolence. No statement can for all time and in all ages adequately express the faith; no theological battle won secures for the church an impregnable position where it can hole up forever. The church is charged with an unremitting task of rethinking and restating the faith.

Two considerations make this especially obvious today. (*a*) We have come to appreciate that propositions of whatever kind are time-conditioned: the consequence is that passage of time, by itself alone, renders less relevant what is earlier said. (*b*) We have become aware of a world in rapid change around us: the consequence is that theology must reckon with this change, understanding that 'the world not only provides opportunities for the communication of the gospel: it also has a hermeneutical function'. Nothing can diminish the certain grandeur of the theology of WCF, or obliterate the beneficial influence it historically exercised; and of course its theological insights can still be didactically used today. But to continue to use it as 'standard' is like NATO matching up to nuclear Russia by bringing up Mons Meg from Edinburgh Castle or mobilizing the Yeoman of the Guard of the Tower of London.

There are some who resist any reassessment of the traditional relationship of Presbyterian churches to WCF, whether by further qualifications in adherence, amendment of text, or official revision of relation. This attitude in fact conflicts with the document they profess to honour: WCF itself affirms that 'all synods may err' (33.3) and that all 'doctrines of men' are subject to judgment by the Spirit speaking in the scripture' (1.10). Study of scripture has led to the detection of serious error in WCF and resulted in the repudiation of several of its key affirmations concerning both belief and practice. The intention of such people is honourable: to defend the faith; the means they propose are disastrous: they prop up a status quo inherited from the past, fearing nothing so much as change. Yet change they cannot escape, for change inescapably suffuses the situation. At the Reformation the church had to engage in infighting. It need and can indulge in this no longer. Its dispute is no longer with itself; its debate is with the world, which, vastly changed and still changing, confronts all the churches with common and equal challenge. The churches have today to devise a common approach to an alienated and incredulous world. To do that they have at least to appear credible.

Time has turned the bright sword of WCF, not into biblical ploughshares, but into historical shackles; what was once a banner is now a totem. The concept of 'standard' and 'subordinate standard' is questionable. The present writer sees it as beyond question that WCF should no longer parade as standard, but recede into the past to which it belongs, and there be given an enhanced because unequivocal place of high honour and limited authority among other historical confessions. This would open the way for up-to-date adherence to scripture itself without the mischievous intervention of a now distorting interpretative prism.

The writer acknowledges indebtedness to Professor G. S. Hendry (*The Westminster Confession for Today* [1960]), and to Professor J. B. Torrance of Aberdeen and the Rev. James Philip of Edinburgh (two unpublished papers).

[1] This was less anomalous then than it seems to us now, for the relation of parliament to Assembly was quite different in the sixteenth and seventeenth centuries: behind even the Scots Confession was a resolution of Parliament 1560 'to produce a statement of the Protestant faith'.

Baptists and Statements of Faith

THE REVEREND W. M. S. WEST, J.P., M.A., D.TH., LL.D.,
PRINCIPAL, BRISTOL BAPTIST COLLEGE

ON the morning of Wednesday, 5 July 1905 the inaugural Congress of the Baptist World Alliance meeting in London heard an address by the President of the Congress, Dr Alexander McLaren. Dr McLaren was one of the foremost preachers amongst English Baptists of the early twentieth century. After reminding the congregation of what he called 'two crystal phrases, which carry everything I want to say – "in the name of Christ", "by the power of the Spirit"', he went on to make this statement:

> I should like that there should be no misunderstanding on the part of the English public, or the American public either – before whom we are taking a prominent position, for a day at any rate – as to where we stand in the continuity of the historic Church. And I should like the first aact of this Congress to be the audible and unanimous acknowledgement of our Faith. So I have suggested that, given your consent, it would be an impressive, and right thing, and would clear away a good deal of slander – if we here and now, in the face of the world, not as a piece of coercion or discipline, but as a simple acknowledgement of where we stand and what we believe, would rise to our feet and following the lead of your President, would repeat the Apostles' Creed. Will you?[1]

The whole gathering then instantly rose and repeated slowly and deliberately, after Dr McLaren, the whole of the Apostles' Creed.

This was a somewhat unusual beginning of this inaugural Congress so far as Baptists were concerned. On the whole, they were not in the habit of using the Apostles' Creed, or any other creed, in worship at that time. It is interesting, however, to note the two reasons that Dr Mclaren gave for the saying together of the Apostles' Creed. It was said, first, to clear away misunderstandings and stop the mouth of slander, and secondly, in order that there could be an acknowledgement of the Faith which Baptists hold. The purpose was both negative and positive. What was true, then, of Baptists and their use of the Creed sums up, probably, the general history of how and why Baptists have used creeds and have indeed written their own confessions of faith. For during the early years of their existence, Baptists did make considerable use of their confessions of faith.

I

The Seventeenth-century Confessions of Faith

When Baptists developed in the early seventeenth century, there stood two groups with somewhat different origins. One group, who became known as the General Baptists, originated amongst Separatist exiles in Holland and tended to be Arminian in theology; the second group, known as the Particular Baptists, who were Calvinistic in outlook, originated in the Separatist stream in London. It was the particular Baptists who in 1644 produced what is really the first comprehensive confession of faith.[2] The motives behind the publication of the 1644 Confession are stated by its signatories in their preface. They claimed that they had been unjustly charged 'both in pulpit and in print' of denying certain doctrines and of holding certain others. They were accused, for example, so they said, of believing in free-will and of denying original sin. They complained further that the effect of these false reports had both alienated the godly and encouraged the ungodly to 'get together in Clusters and stone us'. Thus the leaders of the congregations decided to publish this confession to establish their Calvinistic orthodoxy. They emphasized that the Confession was signed by the representatives of seven congregations, thus making it clear that it was not the judgment of one congregation on its own. The motivation is evident, to confess what they do believe and to deny false accusations concerning what they are said to believe.

The General Baptists in 1651 published a confession of faith (*BCF*, 171-188) representing the belief of thirty congregations in Leicestershire, Lincolnshire, and adjoining counties. This confession of faith like others which appeared during the period of the Commonwealth (1650-1659) often served as an instrument of unification among Baptist congregations. They felt the need to stand together and they took the opportunity of making evident their unity in faith. During the Commonwealth period the Midlands was a principal area of Baptist faith, particularly the General Baptists.

This Confession has its purpose stated very clearly immediately following the title. It says, 'Published (in love) by consent of two from each congregation appointed for that purpose (1) To inform those who have a desire to know what religious duties they hold forth. (2) To undeceive those that are misinformed thereof. (3) To the end that the said congregations may in love and the spirit of meekness, be informed by any that conceive they walk amiss' (*BCF*, 174).

In 1656 the Particular Baptists in Somerset issued their own confession of faith. This seems to have originated, so the Epistle Dedicatory states, in order that the Somerset churches may be seen to share agreement with the London churches and to bear a witness for the Lord. But it is also apparent that the confession of faith in Somerset in 1656 is not unrelated to the considerable pressure being put upon the Baptist churches in the West at this time by the Quakers. W. L. Lumpkin suggests also that this confession 'probably represents an attempt to comprehend all Baptists of the district irrespective of their Calvinism and Arminianism' (*BCF*, 203).

'A brief Confession or Declaration of faith' was set forth by the General Baptists in 1660 in London (*BCF*, 219-235). The purpose of this was to inform all of their innocent belief and practice and then the signatories add 'for which we are not only resolved to suffer persecution, to a loss of our goods, but also life itself, rather than to decline the same' (*BCF*, 224). According to Crosby, the eighteenth-century Baptist historian, this particular confession was signed by representatives of more than twenty thousand General Baptists throughout the United Kingdom.[3] It may be that this company of Baptists was anxious to persuade Charles II upon his restoration to England that they were law-abiding and not anarchist Anabaptists.

In 1677 the Particular Baptists issued a further confession of faith known as the Second London Confession of Particular Baptists (*BCF*, 235-295). This confession follows very closely the Westminster Confession, and is concerned, like so many of the confessions that we have noticed, to seek to ensure that the readers recognize how the Baptists stand firmly and squarely with the Presbyterians and others in their general beliefs, departing only on the issue of baptism. A similar creed, the so-called 'Orthodox Creed' of the General Baptists, was adopted in 1678, which also kept very close to the Westminster Confession, but is of particular interest for our purpose in that it contains a article on the three Creeds (BCF , 295-334). Article 38 runs as follows:

Of the three Creeds –
The three creeds, viz. Nicene creed, Athanasius's creed, and the Apostles' creed,

as they are commonly called, ought thoroughly to be received, and believed. For we believe, they may be proved, by most undoubted authority of holy scripture, and are necessary to be understood of a christians; and to be instructed in the knowledge of them, by the ministers of Christ, according to the analogy of faith, recorded in sacred scriptures, upon which these creeds are grounded, and catechistically opened, and expounded in all christian families, for the edification of young and old, which might be a means to *prevent heresy* in doctrine, and practice, these *creeds* containing all things in a brief manner, that are necessary to be known, fundamentally, in order to our salvation; to which end they may be considered, and better understood of all men, we have here printed them under their several titles as followeth, viz. . . .

(BCF, 326)

There then follow the three Creeds printed in full.

So far the confessions of faith have assumed that the basic point of reference for faith and action was the Bible, and indeed in the creed of 1660 there is a specific article No. 23 that says 'that the Holy Scriptures is the rule whereby saints, both in matters of faith and conversation, are to be regulated . . .' (*BCF*, 232). The confessions reflect this clear assumption that the scriptures contain all that is necessary for the faith and action of the Baptist believer. But in the 1678 creed there is recognition of the part to be played by the traditional creeds of the church, but clearly as aids to the understanding of the biblical truths.

R. G. Torbet sums up the purposes of Baptist confessions of faith in the seventeenth century under five points:

1. To maintain purity of doctrine.
2. To clarify and validate the Baptist position.
3. To serve as a guide to the General Assembly or local Association in advising churches.
4. To serve as a basis for fellowship within local churches, associations or a General Assembly.
5. To discipline churches and members.[4]

It is particularly important to note that this fifth use of the confessions is not to suggest that they are credal tests to be accepted literally word for word, and the confessions of faith were certainly not an attempt to force conformity in the absolute sense. The Baptist practice has been that when there has been a question of doctrinal difficulty, then the local Baptist church would withdraw fellowship from those whose doctrine might prove harmful to the accepted teaching of churches in the Baptist fellowship. This point is of particular importance because Baptists have, from the beginning, always been deeply concerned for the individual's freedom of religious practice and belief in the sight of God. There may be disagreement with an individual which will require the rest of the fellowship withdrawing fellowship from that person, but there remains the right of that individual to hold his own particular belief. There is no doubt that the 1677 Confession of the Particular Baptists took over from the Westminster Confession with very deep conviction the article on liberty of conscience which reads:

> God alone is Lord of the conscience and hath left it free from the doctrines and commandments of men which are in anything contrary to His word, or not contained in it. So that to believe such doctrines, or obey such commands out of conscience is to betray true liberty of conscience; and the requiring of an implicit Faith, and absolute and blind obedience, is to destroy liberty of conscience and reason also.

(*BCF*, 279)

II

The Eighteenth Century

With the coming of William and Mary to the throne and the granting of tolerance to the Baptists and others in England in 1688, the necessity for confessions of faith among Baptists seems to have lessened. The eighteenth century saw a growing questioning of the need for confessions of faith and also of the adequacy particularly of the ancient creeds of the church and even of the Reformation creeds. It has to be remembered particularly that subscription to the ancient creeds could be required still as a test for entry to the universities and to public office. This seemed to Baptists to be an infringement of the liberty of conscience of the individual as well as one of the signs of a continuing oppressive establishment in the church. A number of local Baptist churches continued to have in their minute books statements of faith but on the whole these were the confessions of usually the first pastor of a church and not that of the church itself. Noticeably, however, as the growth of the movement of churches associating together in what the Baptists know as the Associations developed in the seventeenth and particularly the eighteenth century most of the Associations set out brief summaries in their beliefs. These declarations were usually brief and, on the whole, broad in conception. They lacked the precision of the seventeenth-century confessions of faith. Nevertheless there is some evidence of a need still felt by at least some Baptists for a confession of faith to set forth the Baptist interpretation of truths contained in the NT. Joshua Thomas of Leominster maintained that such a confession of faith was necessary 'to make it clear whether we were Unitarians or Trinitarians, Calvinists or Arminians, believers in baptism by immersion on the ground of faith or otherwise'.[5] Others argued against this point of view. The contrary argument suggested that if a confession contained more that the NT it would contain too much. If it contained less, it would be too little. If it only contained the same, it would be superfluous. The danger was felt that the confessions could be made as was said 'millstones and not milestones'. More and more there was the appeal simply to the Bible and, it has to be said, particularly to the NT as the touchstone of the Baptists for their doctrine.

III

The growth of the Baptist Union and its basis of Faith

In the nineteenth century there came into being the Baptist Union which was a Union in a very general sense of the word, of a number of Particular Baptist churches. The old General Baptist had tended very much in the eighteenth century to move into Unitarianism and it was mainly the Particular Baptists who continued the Baptist witness. A number of Particular Baptist churches decided in 1813 to relate together in a Union. The initial Constitution of the Union began with what can only be called a very brief but pithy Confession of Faith. In view of subsequent history of the Baptist Union's basis it is perhaps worth quoting in full:

> The General Union of Baptist Ministers and Churches maintaining the important doctrines of three equal Persons in the Godhead; eternal and personal election; original sin; particular redemption; free justification by the imputed righteousness of Christ; efficacious grace in regeneration; the final perseverance of real believers; the resurrection of the dead; the future judgment; the eternal happiness of the righteous, and the eternal misery of such as die in impenitence, with the congregation order of the churches inviolably.[6]

This doctrinal statement was clearly intended to define what may be taken as 'the soundness of the faith'. In 1832 there was a revision of the Constitution which greatly abbreviated the previous Constitution, startlingly so, so far as the doctrinal declaration of 1813 is concerned. The first clause of the Constitution now simply reads:

To extend brotherly love and union among the Baptist ministers and churches who agree in the sentiments usually denominated evangelical.

(*BU*, 61)

The contrast is remarkable. Of course the 1813 doctrinal declaration had the then familiar Calvinistic pattern. It may well be that the drafters of the 1832 Constitution had in mind the possible adherence of churches belonging to what was called The New Connexion of Baptist Churches. This New Connexion came into being in 1770 and was of General Baptist persuasion. From 1832 onwards until the present day, off and on, there has been pressure for there to be a far more detailed credal statement as the basis of the Baptist Union. In 1873 the basis of the Union was altered. The reference to 'evangelical sentiments' was removed and in its place there was submitted a Declaration of Principle which, it may be argued, said even less specifically. It reads:

In this Union it is fully recognized that every separate church has liberty to interpret and administer the laws of Christ and that the immersion of believers is the only Christian baptism.

(*BU*, 109)

Dr E. A. Payne comments: 'The dropping of the older phrase caused regrets in certain quarters and awakened suspicions. . . . On the other hand by 1873 the phrase had become ambiguous and was liable to misrepresentation and misuse. The new formula was felt to safeguard the independence of the churches against anything approaching synodal action on the part of the Union. By removing any attempt at a credal definition, the fellowship of "strict" and "open" communion churches was maintained, as well as making easier that between those with Calvinistic and Arminian trust deeds' (*BU*, 110).

In 1887-88 the Baptist Union suffered greatly in a controversy which is known as the 'Downgrade Controversy'. In the controversy, difficulties arose in connexion with the Baptist Union and the great Baptist preacher C. H. Spurgeon and others. There was an accusation that the Baptist Union contained those who were less than orthodox. Possibly had there been within the declaration of the Union a stronger doctrinal statement, this controversy might have been avoided, but certainly by the turn of the century it was felt that the basis of the Union needed to be looked at. In October 1904 a new Declaration of Principle was re-phrased as follows.

> The Basis of this Union is:
> 1. That our Lord Jesus Christ is the sole and absolute authority in all matters pertaining to faith and practice, as revealed in the Holy Scriptures, and that each Church has liberty to interpret and administer His laws.
> 2. That Christian Baptism is the immersion in water, into the Name of the Father, the Son and Holy Ghost, of those who have professed repentance toward God and faith in our Lord jesus Christ. Who 'died for our sins according to the Scriptures; was buried, and rose again the third day'.
> 3. That it is the duty of every disciple to bear personal witness to the Gospel of Jesus Christ, and to take part in the evangelization of the world.
>
> (*BU*, 162)

In 1906 the Declaration was altered by the addition of the words 'Our God and Saviour' in the first section after the words 'Our Lord Jesus Christ' (*BU*, 162). This was perhaps an attempt to exclude any Unitarian interpretation of the Person of Christ. This basis of the Union did in fact move, of course, towards the concept of some very brief though real confession of faith.

In 1938 two further changes were made to the Declaration of Principle which were intended to strengthen it doctrinally. The phrase 'Our Lord and Saviour Jesus Christ, God manifest in the flesh' replaced 'The Lord Jesus Christ, our God and Saviour'. In the last section of the first part of the Declaration the liberty of each church to interpret and administer the laws was now declared to be 'under the guidance of the Holy Spirit' (*BU*, 212). Thus the basis of the Baptist Union is now still this simple yet real doctrinal affirmation. We shall return in a moment to a consideration of such pressures as at present exist for the alteration again of this basis.

IV

Ecumenical Responses

But the Union had not only to be concerned with its own affairs during the latter part of the nineteenth century. It also had been challenged by the approaches that were made to the churches in England by the Church of England itself. On 10 April 1889 the Archbishop of Canterbury had addressed a letter to the President of the Baptist Union, the Reverend Dr J. Clifford, inviting a consideration as 'to what steps can be taken, either towards corporate reunion, or towards such relations as may prepare the way for fuller organic unity hereafter' (quoted *BU*, 272). It was this letter that contained what became known as the Lambeth Quadrilateral with its four points, namely: the acceptance of the Holy Scriptures, the acceptance of the Apostles' Creed and the Nicene Creed, the acceptance of the two sacraments, and the acceptance of the historic episcopate. For our purpose we may note that the Baptist Union replied in the autumn of 1889 indicating how much they agreed with the supreme authority of the Holy Scripture but indicating that the other three articles laid down in the encyclical letter contained terms 'so obviously susceptible of two or more interpretations that they do not seem to us to promise a profitable issue to any deliberations founded upon them' (*BU*, 273). This did not make specific reference to the attitude to the Creeds, but when a further approach was made from the Lambeth Conference of 1920 in 'The appeal to all Christian People' the Baptist Union carefully reflected on this approach with its amended four points and the reply of the Union comments as follows:–

> The Scriptures, in and through which the spirit of God speaks, possess for us supreme and unique authority. While we recognize the historic value of ancient Creeds, we cannot give them a place of authority comparable with that of the Scriptures.

> (*BU*, 280)

This may indicate a rather more open attitude to the question of the Creeds. As was stated at the outset of this article, the Baptists did not have any difficulty, apparently, in following the lead of Dr Alexander McLaren in 1905 in affirming the Apostles' Creed. Thus it was not the contents of the Creed that concerned the Baptists, for they had always, and still do, claim 'as their heritage, the great central stream of Christian doctrine and piety through the centuries'.[7] The difficulty with creeds, and perhaps it may be said the fear about creeds, is that they will become forced upon Baptists as a test of orthodoxy. There was also a continuing fear that they should in some way be thought to be of equal authority with the scriptures.

In 1950 there was published the document *Church Relations in England* which represented the outcome of discussions between representatives of the Archbishop of Canterbury and representatives of the Evangelical Free Churches of England following on the sermon preached by the Archbishop of Canterbury in 1946 in Cambridge. Baptists shared fully in the conversations which led to the production of the 1950 Report and there is no doubt that they were amongst those who shared in the discussion on the use of creeds which took place in those talks. The conclusion of the section on the creeds in the *Church Relations in England* report reads as follows:-

> All Communions acknowledge the Scriptures as the rule and standard of life and faith. There are divergencies with regard to the degree of authority to be attached to Creeds and formularies. It is to be noted, however, that those Communions that maintain an objection of official subscription to Creeds are prepared, when the occasion arises, to make their own Declaration of Faith.[8]

There is little doubt that the Baptist participants would be amongst those referred to in the final sentence of that paragraph. The Baptist Union made its own reply to the 1950 Report in 1953 and in this reply it did make comments on the issue of the creeds. The Baptist reply quoted with favour and agreement the declaration of the 1950 Report that 'On the doctrines of God the Father, the Person and work of Christ, the Person and mission of the Holy Spirit, the Trinity, and the Life Everlasting, we have found nothing which separates any one of these Communions from another. All acknowledge the apostolic faith as contained in the Scriptures and expressed in the Apostles' and Nicene Creeds' (*BU*, 293). However, in a footnote to the Baptist reply, these words occur: 'Baptists are among those who object to formal subscription to Creeds on the grounds set out in the report. We note with satisfaction that those engaged in the conversations were agreed that "the Holy Scriptures contain sufficiently all doctrine required of necessity for eternal salvation through Jesus Christ"' (*BU*, 293). The objections to formal subscriptions which the Church Relations Report tables are that:

> 1. Creeds are a human construction, bearing the marks of the age to which they belong, and, as compared with the authority of Scriptures, have a subordinate and secondary character.

2. They promote a legalistic outlook.

3. They intend to inhibit liberty of interpretation.

4. They become a source of division.

5. They appear to emphasize the faith as a body of doctrine at the expense of faith as a personal act.

(*BU*, 27)

Probably in these five points we find as well stated as anywhere the apprehension that Baptists have felt and still feel about the use of creeds.

From what has been written, it may appear that there are two strands within Baptist thinking, one which insists on the primacy of scripture and sees creeds as an unnecessary addition, and the other which recognizes the need for confessions of faith as a proper interpretation of the biblical authority. Paradoxically the actual position is simpler and yet more complex than that. Although it is impossible to speak with certainty for all Baptists one may hazard certain conclusions.

1. All Baptists accept the Bible as the supreme authority for doctrine and practice.

2. A growing number of Baptists are content to use the classic creeds of the church in worship as community confessions of faith. This is particularly true of the Apostles' Creed and rather less true of the Nicene Creed. But all (or almost all!) Baptists would resist the notion that the classic creeds should be enforced as doctrinal standards upon Christians.

3. There is some pressure now, however, for the production of a modern Baptist 'Confession of Faith' reminiscent of the seventeenth-century confessions which would not only set forth what Baptists believe but could be used also as a test of orthodoxy for Baptists.

Thus there are some who suggest that the Baptist Union Declaration of Principle should be further strengthened doctrinally and become both a confession of faith and a touchstone of orthodox Baptist thought. Many others resist such pressure fearing that the attempt even to produce such a doctrinal statement would be not only divisive but also unnecessary in the light of scripture, and that the use of it might well infringe the liberty of interpretation for the individual conscience which Baptists prize so highly. Which voice will prevail, only time will tell.

[1] *Report of the First Baptist World Congress* [1905], 20.

[2] Text in W. L. Lumpkin: *Baptist Confessions of Faith* (Chicago [1959]), 153-171 (cited as *BCF*). See also B. R. White: 'The Doctrine of the Church in the Particular Baptist Confession of 1644' in *Journal of Theological Studies*, NS XIX [1968], 570-590.

[3] T. Crosby: *A History of the England Baptists* (London [1739]), Vol. II, Appendix IV, 90.

[4] R. G. Torbet: *A History of the Baptists* (Valley Forge [1963]), 45.

[5] *Baptist Quarterly*, NS VII, No. 2 [1934], 60. Quoted in an article, 'The Baptists and the New Testament', by Professor J. G. Jenkins.

[6] E. A. Payne: *The Baptist Union: A Short History* (London [1958]), 24 (cited as *BU*).

[7] Quoted from: 'A Statement approved by the Council of the Baptist Union of Great Britain and Ireland' [March 1948]. Text in *BU*, 283.

[8] *Church Relations in England* (SPCK), 28.

Methodist Statements

THE REVEREND A. RAYMOND GEORGE, M.A., B.D.,
BRISTOL

THE doctrinal standards for Methodist preachers in Great Britain are John Wesley's Notes upon the New Testament and some of his sermons. At present the question of authority in matters of doctrine is one of great interest in many churches, so that even the precise wording of the phrases which refer to a doctrinal standard is often of importance, and the history of Methodism illustrates several interesting points of this kind. Fresh religious bodies in their youthful vigour often feel no need to define their doctrines, until they are forced to do so by the legal issues arising from the possession of property. Thus in 1763 John Wesley published a model deed for his preaching-houses in which it was provided that persons appointed by the Conference of his preachers should 'preach no other doctrine than is contained in Mr Wesley's Notes upon the New Testament, and four volumes of sermons'. The former are easily identified as *Explanatory Notes upon the New Testament* by John Wesley, published in London in 1755 and in numerous subsequent editions. The sermons were not so easy to identify, as there were various editions of them. The phrase itself was later altered to 'the first four volumes of sermons', and there were other minor variations. Eventually the Wesleyan Conference obtained Counsel's opinion and in 1914 recorded the judgment that the phrase refers to the first four volumes of a particular edition, forty-four in number. It had previously been thought that fifty-three sermons were meant.[1]

In 1784 Wesley published a service-book for the Methodists of North America. It was largely an abridgement of the Prayer Book, and similarly concluded with Articles of Religion, reduced from thirty-nine to twenty-four, to which one more was subsequently added. The reduction was partly due to Wesley's passion for abridgement, but there were also some changes in doctrinal emphasis. They became part of the doctrinal standards of Methodism in America, but not in Britain.

It would take too long to trace the history of the standards in all the branches into which Methodism split, but the present Methodist Church in Great Britain is based on the Deed of Union of 1932. This contains the following passage:

> *Doctrine.* The doctrinal standards of the Methodist Church are as follows:
>
> The Methodist Church claims and cherishes its place in the Holy Catholic Church which is the Body of Christ. It rejoiçes in the inheritance of the Apostolic Faith and loyally accepts the fundamental principles of the historic creeds and of the Protestant Reformation. It ever remembers that in the Providence of God Methodism was raised up to spread Scriptural Holiness through the land by the proclamation of the Evangelical faith and declares its unfaltering resolve to be true to its Divinely appointed mission.
>
> The Doctrines of the Evangelical Faith which Methodism has held from the beginning and still holds are based upon the Divine revelation recorded in the Holy Scriptures. The Methodist Church acknowledges this revelation as the supreme rule of faith and practice. These Evangelical Doctrines to which the Preachers of The Methodist Church both Ministers and laymen are pledged are contained in Wesley's Notes on the New Testament and the first four volumes of his sermons.
>
> The Notes on the New Testament and the 44 sermons are not intended to impose a system of formal or speculative theology on Methodist Preachers, but to set up standards of preaching and belief which should secure loyalty to the fundamental truths of the Gospel of Redemption and ensure the continued witness of the Church to the realities of the Christian experience of salvation.[2]

A certain air of cautious vagueness may perhaps be detected in these paragraphs. The historic creeds are not defined, though one may guess that the Apostles' and Nicene Creeds are meant. It is not clear what are their 'fundamental principles', still less those of the Protestant Reformation. The reference to the Holy Scriptures is qualified by the words 'Divine revelation recorded in', and a whole paragraph is devoted to qualifying the reference to the Notes and the Sermons.

There follow five paragraphs about the ministry and one about the sacraments. They have the appearance of being a compromise and have caused some controversy, particularly the following sentences: 'Christ's Ministers in the Church are Stewards in the household of God and Shepherds of His flock. Some are called and ordained to this sole occupation . . .' and 'The Methodist Church . . . believes that no priesthood exists which belongs exclusively to a particular order or class of men . . .'

An important question about any church is whether it claims that its statements of doctrine are irreformable. The churches which united in 1932 took steps to make them so; it was at their request that the Methodist Church Union Act, 1929, section 8, which authorized the union, laid it down that the Conference should have no power to alter or vary the doctrinal clauses, and the Deed of Union itself therefore had a clause to that effect, though adding 'The Conference shall be the final authority within the Methodist Church with regard to all questions concerning the interpretation of its doctrines' (CPD, 547 and Deed of Union, clause 31; CPD, 62 (1977)). But years later the Conference took the view that a church should be master in its own house. The majority would probably have argued that no form of words should be regarded as unalterable, if only because of cultural changes. Whether or not the substance of doctrine should be alterable, at least it might be desirable to alter the verbal expression of it in a way which might go beyond mere interpretation. If such issues were ever to be debated, it would be better for the church to have the right to determine them rather than that an application should have to be made to Parliament. It might be added that no church could use its property for a purpose utterly contrary to the wishes of its founders, for the Charity Commissioners would intervene. This view met with opposition from those who feared alterations of the doctrinal clauses. But after considerable discussion in parliamentary committees the Conference secured the Methodist Church Act 1976, which repealed the Act of 1929, and extended the power of the Conference to amend the Deed of Union so as to cover all its clauses, but with special safeguards 'if the doctrinal standards are thereby affected' (Methodist Church Act, 1976, clause 5, in *CPD*, 10-11 (1976A)).

Is a preacher to be judged by what he believes in his mind or by what he says when he preaches? The old model deed of the Methodist Church had provided that no one was to be permitted to preach 'who shall maintain promulgate or teach any Doctrine or Practice' contrary to the Notes and Sermons (*CPD* [51969], 297). The word 'maintain' is somewhat ambiguous, and though no one would defend insincerity, it seemed better to have a plainly external test in defining the duties of the trustees in regard to permitting people to preach. The new Act avoids this difficulty by saying that the managing trustees, subject to certain exceptions for occasional joint services and for shared buildings, shall not permit anyone 'so to preach or expound God's Holy Word or perform any act as to deny or repudiate the doctrinal standards' (Methodist Church Act, 1976, Schedule 2, clause 14 (3) in *CPD*, 82 (1976A)).

Yet whereas the trustees are to employ this negative test, those who are to be authorized to preach must themselves express their belief in a positive way. Thus before anyone is admitted as a local preacher he must pass an examination 'as to his knowledge of and loyalty to the following doctrines of the evangelical faith, namely the fatherhood of God, the deity of our Lord Jesus Christ, the person, mission and work of the Holy Spirit, the universality of sin, the atonement, salvation for all by grace through faith, the believer's privilege of assurance and of perfect love, the Christian church, the future life' (*CPD*, 272). It is then stated that these doctrines are based upon the Holy Scriptures and are contained in Wesley's Notes and Sermons. A candidate for the ministry must before nomination assent to the doctrinal standards; at ordination he must answer the question 'Do you believe the doctrines of the Christian faith as this Church has received them?' and annual inquiry is made at the Ministerial Sessions of the Synod 'Does he believe and preach our doctrines?' (*CPD*, 310 (1977), *The Methodist Service Book* [1975], G9, *CPD*, 400 (1979)).

As in many other churches a different test is applied to members. The condition of membership in Wesley's day, when Methodism was a group of societies rather than a church, was 'a desire to flee from the wrath to come, to be saved from their sins'. The corresponding sentence now begins 'All those who confess Jesus Christ as Lord and Saviour' (*CPD*, 63).

Methodism is unique in thus using a commentary on the Bible and a collection of sermons as its standards. Just as the reformation confessions (including, for this purpose, the Thirty-nine Articles) differ from the creeds in style, length and purpose, so the standards differ from the confessions. The standards resemble the confessions in that they are intended for preachers and are not recited liturgically, but they are much longer and have a different style, which corresponds to their original purpose. They are rightly called standards, by which preaching is to be judged, and this is derived from the origin of Methodism, not as a separate denomination, but as a preaching mission. The Notes, traditionally mentioned first, are a commentary on the NT, a fact which points to the primacy of the scriptures: and the Notes are clearly a *subordinate* standard, though Methodism does not use the phrase. Such standards are necessary because all the great heretics have claimed to be loyal to the Bible. If a church is to have coherence, there must be limits to the ways in which its preachers are allowed to interpret the Bible. The use of the Sermons as a second subordinate standard further emphasizes the characteristic ethos of Methodism. It has often been remarked that in practice the Methodist people learn their theology more from Charles Wesley's hymns than from John Wesley's sermons, but the hymns would be less appropriate as a standard.

What do these standards contain? The Notes are not altogether original; their preface expresses indebtedness to Bengel's *Gnomon*, Heylun, Guyse, and Doddridge. Though the accompanying translation sometimes correctly anticipates the Revised Version, the Notes of course antedate the present style of biblical criticism. Many modern Methodists make little use of them or at best maintain that the proper way to 'read' a commentary is to consult it as needed; yet the most careful modern student of Wesley's christology, comparing the Notes with the Articles and the Sermons, says 'The Notes are, by far, the most fruitful source for Wesley's Christology'.[3] In any case, a conscientious preacher needs to read them in order to know to what doctrine he is assenting.

In the Preface to the Sermons, published in 1746, Wesley says that they contain the substance of his preaching between eight and nine years last past, which means since his heartwarming experience in Aldersgate on 24 May 1738. He designed 'plain truth for plain people'; he endeavoured to set down what he found in the Bible concerning the way to heaven; to describe 'the true, the scriptural, experimental religion, so as to omit nothing which is a real part thereof, and to add nothing thereto which is not' (Sugden, *op. cit.*, I, 29, 30, 32).

The main doctrines in the sermons are the soteriological doctrines which are known in a believer's experience. Methodists often say that they hold the universal Christian faith and have no distinctive doctrines, but only distinctive emphases; but they are equally fond of using the phrase 'our doctrines', by which they mean 'those truths of salvation which are set forth in the Methodist doctrinal standards' (cf. *CPD*, 400 (1979)). They are often set out in this form, sometimes known as the Methodist quadrilateral:

All need to be saved,
All can be saved,
All can know that they are saved,
All can be saved to the uttermost.

It can easily be seen that these correspond to the phrases quoted above in the summary of Methodist doctrine: 'the universality of sin, . . . salvation for all by grace through faith, the believer's privilege of assurance and of perfect love', and it is easy to find sermons corresponding to them, for example, the sermons on Original Sin, Salvation by Faith, The Witness of the Spirit, and Christian Perfection. They are to some extent the common beliefs of Christians but each has been challenged or itself stands in opposition to some particular view. The first is opposed to the Pelagian heresy. The second is directed against Calvinism or at least the extreme form of it; Wesley does not mean that all men are saved (universalism), but that all men can be saved if they have faith. The third has sometimes been attacked as leading to presumptiousness or caricatured as meaning 'salvation by feeling', and the last seems opposed to the widespread Protestant view that a justified man is necessarily at the same time a sinner. When carefully studied, however, it is found to be so carefully qualified as to be compatible with its supposed opposite; in some hands indeed it dies the death of a thousand qualifications. All depends on the definition of 'sin'.

Wesley's doctrine has thus been described as Evangelical Arminianism, a combination which in his day seemed unusual. He was an evangelical, saying that all men, being sinners, need God's grace if they are to be saved. Not all men accept this grace. This might be due, as in Calvinism, to the divine decrees, predestining some to salvation, others to damnation. If, rejecting Calvinism, we take the Arminian view that salvation is offered to all, how are we to account for the fact that some accept it and others reject it? We may say that those who accept it do so by prevenient grace, but as that also is presumably offered to all, the problem remains. Are we not driven to say that those who accept it are better than the rest, that their acceptance of it is meritorious? In that case we have departed from our evangelical starting-point and are tending to a Pelagian denial of man's sinfulness and dependence. The Wesleyan reply may be summed up in a familiar illustration: a man is no less a beggar because he stretches out his hand to receive the gift. The relation of grace to freewill is always mysterious, but Wesley has shown that it is possible to be an Arminian without being a Pelagian.

That this line of argument seems to us fairly obvious is some indication of Wesley's achievement; in his day it was more original. Before Wesley Arminianism had been a mark of high and dry churchmen, whereas those of evangelical or 'low' churchmanship were usually Calvinists. Wesley had at first been a high churchman; after his experience he retained the Arminianism and the high sacramental views of that school, but he also acquired many of the beliefs of the evangelicals; hence his Evangelical Arminianism. Today in all churches few theologians would maintain a rigid Calvinism; it is not so clear that all would wish to be called evangelicals, but many of the characteristics of that view are shared by diverse schools of thought. One might almost say that all are now Evangelical Arminians.

Yet when we look at evangelicals today, in the more 'party' sense of that word, whether in the Church of England or in the non-Methodist Free Churches, they still have a persisting Calvinist 'tone', even though they are no longer rigid Calvinists. It is arguable that it is still Methodism which best exemplifies Evangelical Arminianism, and the role which it now has among the Free Churches, it might in other circumstances have fulfilled as a group within the Church of England.

Another description of Wesley's achievement was that his doctrine is 'an original and unique synthesis of the Protestant ethic of grace with the Catholic ethic of holiness'.[4] The word 'ethic' is unfortunate, and like the former description, this is a broad generalization. Nevertheless it is true that other Protestants have so laid the emphasis on justification by grace through faith and on imputed righteousness that they have not always said enough about sanctification and imparted righteousness, whereas 'Catholics' have been in some danger of laying more emphasis on the human pursuit of sanctity than on the grace of God. Wesley combined the two.

The Sermons are not devoted to the less experienced doctrines of the faith, as for instance, to quote the official list 'the fatherhood of God, the deity of our Lord Jesus Christ, the person, mission and work of the Holy Spirit, . . . the atonement, . . . the Christian Church, the future life'. Yet the mission and work of the Holy Spirit are so intimately connected with the individual's experience that some have maintained that one of the distinctive notes of Methodism is the emphasis on the work of the Holy Spirit. Obviously the doctrines of God the Father, of Christ, and of the atonement are the essential basis of soteriology. Wesley takes these doctrines for granted, and though he does not devote whole sermons to them, they are mentioned or implied frequently enough for us to know that he does not for a moment doubt them and to discern in what style he formulates them.

None of the Standard Sermons deals directly with the church, but there are notable sermons on the Means of Grace and on Catholic Spirit. When these, together with the teaching on Baptism in that on The New Birth, are related to the soteriological teaching, they show that he combined the best of the pietist and Moravian teaching with good churchmanship. The sermon that deals with the future life, that on The Great Assize, falls outside the standard forty-four.

What is perhaps at first sight surprising is that there are no fewer than thirteen sermons on the Sermon on the Mount, as well as three about various aspects of the Law, and some on practical issues such as The Use of Money. These reinforce the teaching on Christian Perfection, and make it abundantly clear that it is possible to be an evangelical without being an antinomian.

Clearly the Sermons are a significant part of the history of Christian doctrine. Wesley despite his professed desire to be a man of one book, *homo unius libri*,[5] read widely, and many influences played on his mind; there has been much recent discussion as to which were the dominant influences, and which were the leading themes in his thought. He is thus often said to have been a synthesizer rather thàn an original thinker; the synthesis itself, however, may claim some originality.

What is their use and significance today? The phrases in the Deed of Union such as 'loyalty to the fundamental truths of the Gospel of Redemption' and 'the realities of the Christian experience of salvation' allow a fairly wide scope, and the very length of the standards makes it implausible to require the kind of detailed assent which a shorter document might be thought to require. The increasing pluralism of theological thought has to some extent affected Methodism, but in Methodism it is not true that 'anything goes'.

The importance the reader will attach to the standard will depend on his theological position. Certainly they need to be supplemented by, or at least interpreted in the light of, biblical, theological, liturgical, and philosophical scholarship, not to mention the behavioural sciences, the comparative study of religion, and so on. But for my part, while avoiding, I hope, the extremes of conservatism, I find that the standards help to keep me close to what I take to be the essential message of the Bible.

[1] The sermons are in *Wesley's Standard Sermons*, edited and annotated by Edward H. Sugden, 2 volumes (London [1921]), which contains an account of this issue in I, 13-16, II, 331-40. A fresh edition of the sermons has begun to appear, edited by A. C. Outler, in the Bicentennial Edition of Wesley's Works (Abingdon Press, Nashville).

[2] The Deed of Union is in *The Constitutional Practice and Discipline of the Methodist Church* (hereafter *CPD*) (London [⁶1974]), 40-67. We cite the Sixth Edition except where otherwise stated. This is clause 30, pp. 61-62 (1977). The year is given in some cases because the work has loose-leaf pages, some of which are later than 1974.

[3] John Deschner, *Wesley's Christology* (Dallas [1960]), 10.

[4] G. C. Cell, *The Rediscovery of John Wesley* (New York [1935]), 347.

[5] Preface to the Sermons in Sugden, *op. cit.*, I, 32.

The Creed and Celebration of Faith in Eastern Orthodox Worship

Dr George H. Bebawi,
St John's College, Nottingham

THE East did not, from the beginning, have one creed. Prior to the famous Nicene-Constantinople creed (hereafter abbreviated to NC), there were different creeds which varied from Alexandria, Jerusalem, Antioch and later Constantinople.[1] These metropolises of the East saw extensive theological debates in the first Christian millennium, from Arianism to Iconoclasm. Aside from that, all the great ecumenical councils also took place in the East and belong historically to the wide range of debate and theology in the area.[2]

All that could have become dead history, but what has made it part of the living reality of the Eastern Orthodox churches is the fact that all this history is embodied in the celebration of the sacraments of the church, worship and the liturgical year. We can see how theology, history and worship are put together in the brilliant way in which the Orthodox liturgy is composed. On the surface, what appears is that prayers, icons and the feasts of the saints are put together in the liturgy, but what becomes obvious on reflection is that history, theology and dogmatic formulae are present as one unit.

In order not to complicate the matter, let us look, for example, at the feasts of some of the Fathers of the church who were present at the ecumenical councils. What we see is the celebration of the testimony of the Fathers to Christian faith and the historical, theological and dogmatic definition of the councils taking place in the eucharistic liturgy. The believers who assemble to receive communion are celebrating not simply what has taken place in the past, but also what is still confessed in the prayers which bear the names of various great saints, such as Basil the Great, John Chrysostom, etc. Scholars may have spent much time proving whether or not, for example, Basil wrote the Greek/Coptic liturgy of Basil, but the fact that his name is attached to a set of prayers means that they are in accord with the faith of the Fathers, as witnessed to by Basil.[3] One can also see that the change of the name of the Liturgy of St Mark to the Liturgy of St Cyril of Alexandria has served the purpose of unifying the Egyptian church in its rejection of the heresy of Nestorius, and later of reinforcing its defence of its christology when the Council of Chalcedon (in 451) was rejected by the Copts. For it is in the liturgy more than anywhere else that the people of God identify themselves as participants in the apostolic tradition and in the struggle of the Fathers of the church against certain heresies. Theology and liturgy are but one unit in which prayer and history are in constant interaction because of the growing number of feasts and what has been added to the liturgical prayers.

If we look carefully we realize that saints and feasts and prayers are the living link with the history of the church. This is not expressed in books but in worship, in the very practice of faith and in the attitude that the life of the church is a continuous witness to the apostolic tradition. But it is also a complicated matter, for while this is done very well to bring forward the richness of the past and to link it with the celebration of the sacraments, the fact is that this has led to complicated ethnic, linguistic and historical developments which have left the Orthodox churches sunk in their rich past, but cut off from the contemporary world. To remedy this, the great dogmatic formulae of the past need to be translated from the ancient languages – Greek, Syriac, Armenian, etc. – not literally, of course, but in concept, so that the message of the Fathers of the church may continue to be conveyed. History can become a trap, both if we simply repeat the words of the past, and if we throw away the formulae of history in favour of a clearer teaching 'suitable' for the present.

The genius of the Orthodox liturgy was to use three important means of expressing Christian faith.

The first is the prayers of the liturgies themselves, which contain a great deal of rich theology. One need not read the Fathers of the church to learn the Orthodox faith. If one simply reads the prayers which are used for the sacraments, especially the eucharist, one learns a lot.

The second means is the various hymns that have been composed during the life of the church. They are numerous and carry with them theology, spirituality and dogmatic definition. It is beyond the scope of this article to explain the history and background of the hymns of the Orthodox churches,[4] but their function is clear. These hymns, which vary from thanksgiving to praise, are based on the dogmatic work of the Fathers. Generations of Orthodox authors transformed what we may consider dry theology into prayers and poetry and put it all in the form of praise. This has closed the gap between theology and worship and made the achievement of the past flow into the life of prayer of the church. The dogmatic formulae become signs that point to grace and help to deepen the relationship between God and his people. This is done for worship rather than in a mere mental speculation which brings that sense of dryness.

One good example is the hymn that is variously attributed to Cyril of Alexandria, Severus of Antioch, or even the emperor Justinian.[5] The fact that all the Orthodox churches, those who rejected the Council of Chalcedon, such as the Copts, the Armenians, the Syrians and the Ethiopians, as well as those who accept it – the Greeks, Russians, etc. – are united in using this hymn, proves its importance. Indeed it became as important as the NC creed itself. To shed light on the function of the hymns, let us look at the words of this famous example:

> O only-begotten Son and Word of God, thou who art immortal yet didst accept for our salvation to become incarnate of the holy Mother of God (Theotokos) and ever-virgin Mary, and wast made man without change; who also wast crucified for us, O Christ our Lord, trampling down death by death; who art one of the Holy Trinity, and art glorified together with the Father and the Holy Spirit: save us.

One could ask what is missing here of the great doctrines of the church and find nothing to answer. Such rich words as these are used in worship and sung by the people at the mystery of the eucharist. Here we can see that theology is celebrated as an essential part of the Christian experience of salvation.

The third means is the word of God in scripture as it is used liturgically. The Bible forms the backbone of the prayers and hymns of the Orthodox churches. That is to say, they contain frequent biblical quotations which means that those who read the Bible or listen to it being read, cannot fail to recognize the various passages that are used in the prayers. Worship unfolds the meaning of many texts and explains how they are understood in the context of the celebration of the sacraments and prayer. The Bible as a book becomes a witness to what is now taking place in the life of the community. It is deeply venerated in the liturgy and remains on the altar all the time to symbolize that the word of God and the sacraments are one reality of the divine love for mankind and must not be separated. This organic unity of the word of God and the sacraments makes worship an important dimension for our understanding of the word of God, as the word of God proclaims what is celebrated by the church.

Perhaps some quotations will clarify this:

> Hail, O Lady, fiery chariot of the Logos;
> O living Paradise, having the Lord, the Tree of life in your midst; whose sweetness gives life to those partaking in faith . . . Receiving the Logos in your womb, you held him who holds all creation in his hands and nourished with milk him who feeds the universe by a quickening nod. O pure one to him we sing, 'Praise the Lord all his works and exalt him throughout all the ages'.[6]

One cannot fail to see how texts and certain events from both testaments have been mingled together: Paradise, the tree of life, the chariot of fire – all that is set with the actual birth of Christ as a baby and his mighty power, which gives life and feeds the universe. Now he is humbled and is fed by the Virgin Mary.

The unity of the Bible is seen in terms of shadow and reality, and of promise and fulfilment. What has taken place in the Old Testament is now fulfilled in the New.

The Function of the Creeds

It is very important to point out that the NC creed was not used until the beginning of the fifth century, for the late homilies of John of Chrysostom in Constantinople around 379 do not allude to it.[7] It is the Nestorian debate 'on the one Lord Jesus Christ' that gave more prominence to the NC, but the local creeds of Alexandria, Jerusalem, Antioch and Constantinople were still in use side by side with it. It is also important to see that the formal, or what we may call official, terminology of Nicaea, including such words as *homoousios*, was not used by

St Basil in his book *On the Holy Spirit* and is similarly absent from the writings of other Fathers.[8] The spirit of the Eastern churches is tolerant of the various ways that lead to truth. This means that truth does not stand or fall because of a word. So for example, the oneness of Father, Son and Holy Spirit does not depend on the Nicaean terminology; one could then ask, and what was the basis for the Nicaean insistence on saying that Christ is of the same substance with the Father, or one substance with the Father? The soteriological background of the *homoousios* must not be neglected in favour of the rigid thorough investigation of history, language and doctrinal development.

It is baptism as the mystery of the divine adoption of mankind in Christ that cuts short the Fathers' arguments with heresies. A quick glance at St Basil's book *On the Holy Spirit* or the earlier work of St Athanasius *Against the Arians* will prove how baptism became the pivot of the Orthodox understanding of Trinity.[9] This in fact proves the pastoral and practical side of the theology of the Fathers and helps us to see that the dogmatic development of the early centuries was not a fight over words, or dependent on the decision of a Council of Nicaea in 325. An evidence of this is the non-appearance of the NC creed in a manuscript as late as the ninth- to tenth-century Barbarini MS, which contains a good collection of the liturgical prayers of the church of Constantinople.[10] St Basil and John Chrysostom used different expressions from those of the NC creed, such as 'sharing the same glory with the Father' or 'like the Father in essence'.[11] This not only gives us different words to express orthodox faith, but also avoids what we may call the church's formal confession of faith.

Yet what is more important is that Christian doctrine is an integral part of the sacramental life of the church. Many scholars would question the link between Christ's birth of the Virgin Mary and the Christian experience of baptism, which is the birth from above of water and the Holy Spirit, but the wholeness of the theology of the Fathers would not allow the split between doctrines and sacraments or between the life of Christ in its totality, from his eternal birth of the Father to his incarnation, crucifixion and second coming, and sacraments and worship. All that has happened to Christ and all that is Christ is the basis for Christian worship, the sacraments, prayer and the spiritual life of the church.

Thus the virgin birth is a type of what takes place in baptism, the coming to birth of a new humanity which is re-created from above and not according to the law of nature (John 1[13]). It is a question not of whether this is history or a myth, but of the grace of God that is given to transform the being of man. This grace is the person of Christ in the sense that he reveals to us our destiny, not in words, but through what takes place in him. If we ask ourselves whether this is history or not, the answer will be that the historicity of the virgin birth of Christ is the basis for the new history of the new humanity. We cannot reject one and accept the other unless we want to separate Christ as the second Adam from those who are redeemed, that is the new humanity. In this sense the creed and the life of the church are so interwoven that no one can understand either without the other.[12]

We also need to remember that the creed was historically speaking, part of the initiation of the catechumens.[13] The creed is an integral part of the sacrament of baptism and if it is separated from it, it loses its function and significance and becomes like a poster that does not convey a message. But it was in the baptismal liturgy that the creed was handed down to the baptized, and it is now recited in the eucharistic celebration.

This is not the place to discuss the relationship between baptism and the eucharist, but what is clear from the eucharistic celebration is that the baptized persons bring along with them to the eucharist, the creed, the Lord's prayer and the grace of adoption. This explains their presence and participation in the banquet of the kingdom of God, that is the Lord's Supper. One can see that the confession of faith in the creed is sacramentally based, liturgically practised and makes past history a celebration in worship to enable the people to learn more about the grace of their adoption. Every baptized Christian in both East and West received at his baptism not only the creed, but also the Lord's prayer. The early church saw in the Lord's prayer the prayer of the baptized, of those who can call God Father and ask for the coming of his kingdom, which was sometimes understood to be the indwelling of the Holy Spirit.

It is important to see that in the commentaries on the Lord's prayer, from the early commentary by Tertullian up to the very late one by St Maximos the Confessor (seventh century), the various articles of the faith are explained. If this points to anything it is to the close link between baptism and the eucharist, as the first gives birth and the second provides nourishment. The creed and the Lord's prayer were given at baptism and their appearance in the eucharistic liturgies means that they convey the message of the grace of adoption as the foundation of our presence at the banquet of the eucharist.

Confession of faith is part of every church meeting, at vespers, matins, weddings, funerals, etc. Although these church services were a later development, it is faith as declared in the NC creed which makes up part of the fabric of the life of the church.

The Creed as Part of Apophatic Theology[14]

It is a mistake to think of the doctrine of the Trinity as an explanation of the nature of Godhead. All the Fathers who defend the Nicaean faith remind us constantly that God's nature is beyond our understanding. The doctrine of the Trinity is therefore to be seen as dealing with salvation rather than with the nature of God. One can read St Athanasius and other Fathers expressing their concern with the oneness of the *ousia* of the Father, Son and Holy Spirit to establish man's participation in the divine nature as the sure way to his salvation.[15] The purpose of the creed is to safeguard the basis of our salvation rather than to explain God to us. If God remains beyond our understanding,[16] then the *homoousios* is a declaration of how God saved man rather than of who God is and what his nature is. The defence of the faith against Arianism was soteriologically rather than philosophically based. As the language of all educated people was Greek, *ousia* and *homoousios* were not words foreign to the dialogue of daily life. Even today, 'essence', the equivalent of *ousia*, is not alien to popular English. Obviously the philosophical aspects of the word related to essence and accident are known only to students of philosophy, but we still talk about essence and cannot drop the word altogether. It is my conviction that the Fathers similarly used the word *ousia* in a popular rather than philosophical way.

A fair and fresh reappraisal will show that at present we usually deal with the texts of the Nicene and post-Nicene Fathers through a late nineteenth- and early twentieth-century understanding of the development of Christian doctrine, which divides Christian theology into Greek and Jewish or Hellenic and Semitic. This division prevents us from penetrating the meaning of the texts to see that what we have is not a Greek way of expressing faith, but a continuation of the biblical

Greek of the Septuagint and the New Testament. The parable of the Lost Son (Luke 15) uses the word *ousia* in a popular sense to mean 'goods', all the lost son had or possessed (verse 13), which is not quantified. God's substance is what God possesses and that certainly means how he revealed that in Christ. It is a way of speaking of the reality of God rather than of speculating about his nature, since God's nature is beyond our understanding.

In that the creed must remain in the stream of apophatic theology as a safeguard for what has been given rather than as an explanation of what is beyond our understanding.

The patristic distinction between *economia* and *theologia* in theology has to be taken seriously by us in modern times.[19] All that belongs to the incarnation and salvation is the main subject of the *economia*, where we see God working. But true *theologia*, our knowledge of God, is to know that we know nothing, or nothing that can be expressed. The two main parts of the NC creed deal with the Son and the Holy Spirit. It says very little about the Father and even the early word 'Trinity' does not occur. The NC creed rather states belief in 'one God' who is creator of heaven and earth. The beginning of Christian faith has always been the creation of the cosmos and of man, rather than the eternal, timeless, unknowable nature of God, which is of no pastoral significance. The Fathers, generally speaking, if we exclude some like Origen and Didymous, were very careful to start from creation, as is seen from the lectures on the Creed of Jerusalem attributed to Cyril of Jerusalem (fourth century) or the earlier works *Contra Gentes* and *De Incarnatione* by Athanasius, where he begins with creation to refute dualism and to explain the Logos' becoming man.[20] We have no speculative theology about the nature of God, but a theology that is geared to the pastoral concern of their time.

This shows that theology without worship is a frame without a picture or a machine that is used for the wrong purpose. But if theology and worship are integrated, we can see that Christian maturity does not start, or indeed end, with an official confession of faith as formulated in a creed – any creed – but with what grows in us guided by a creed, prayer, the word of God, hymns and the sacraments. Our relationship with God has to be guided, but guided by celebration, not by the imposition of a particular form of confession which becomes an obligation.

Apophatic theology, if taken seriously, leads us to see that forms of words, texts, hymns, etc. are signs that guide us to the knowledge of the mystery of God, which is above all forms and words.[17] God is revealed in Christ, but that is a mystery. The Son is both very God and very man, but no form of dogmatic definition reveals the mystery of God in Christ; the definitions rather warn us against heretical understandings of the mystery. Here the liturgical prayers of the great feasts, such as Christmas, Good Friday, etc., as celebrated by the Orthodox churches, provide the best kind of support for the NC creed; in them believers are reminded of the paradox of the mystery of God in Christ who is so near and so far, touchable but unknowable, in us but beyond our grasp.[18] The creed belongs to liturgical celebration and to what goes with it – the hymns, the prayers, the feasts and the sacraments. These developed together slowly over centuries, never aiming at defining the mystery of God, but taking the course of avoiding the heresies.

But if we ask ourselves what would the confession of faith have been if there had never been heresies, the answer is that the creeds of the local churches of the East would have survived and remained part of the celebration of both baptism and the eucharist.

On the other hand, we need to examine very carefully the teaching of the church on the Trinity, incarnation and the Holy Spirit outside the anti-heretical writings in the ascetic writings and liturgical prayers. We can see that these have not escaped the influence of the dogmatic vocabulary that developed after the ecumenical councils and especially that which was current at the time of their composition, but the positive message of the doctrine, which reveals the relationship between God and man in Christ, can nevertheless be seen. The merit of apophatic theology is in its attempt to transcend all forms, formulae and images. This keeps the way wide open for the positive side of faith proclaimed by the creed. But the weak side of apophatic theology is that, by its very nature, it ultimately becomes impossible to teach.

The Confession of Faith in the Eastern Churches Today

The Eastern churches have not managed to avoid the ongoing debate between the Roman and Reformed churches that has taken place since the sixteenth century. Although all Orthodox churches from the seventeenth century onwards followed Latin theology and often copied without discrimination what Roman theologians have produced,[21] a fresh examination of the Eastern tradition was going on at the same time in Russia among Russian theologians. The Bolshevik Revolution in 1917 disrupted the revival of interest in the holistic perception of the Fathers of theology, worship, sacraments and asceticism, but there is much hope in some Orthodox theological colleges which have recaptured the spirit of the Fathers.

Most modern Orthodox catechisms are based on the questions, answers, problems and models of thinking that developed in the West.[22] The syncretistic style of these books is obvious; they use both Protestant and Catholic vocabulary and concepts. The NC creed has become the only recognized creed, to the extent that the Apostles' Creed, which has been in use in the Western churches for centuries, is ignored because it was not known in the East. It shares the fate of the old Eastern creeds. But beneath the official voice of the Orthodox churches there remains the voice of the theologians and the laity, who explain their faith from the experience of the mystery of God in Christ as celebrated in the liturgy. They are less restrained by the official formulae that have dominated theological books since the eighteenth century.

[1] For the Greek text of the creeds of Alexandria and other Eastern metropolises, see T. H. Brindley, *The Ecumenical Documents of the Faith* (London [1906]), 57-69. Also the best book available in English: J. N. D. Kelly, *Early Christian Creeds* (London [1950]), 131-201.

[2] For the basic definitions of faith, see W. A. Hammond, *Definitions of Faith* (Oxford [1843]) and J. Stevenson, *Creeds, Councils and Controversies* (London [1966]).

[3] J. Fenwick, *Fourth Century Anaphoral Construction Techniques* (Grove Liturgical Study 45, Nottingham [1986]), which gives the up-to-date views on the Anaphora of St Basil (pp. 6-10).

[4] A good and brief discussion of the history of the hymns of the Byzantine Church is given in J. Savas, *Hymnology of the Eastern Orthodox Church* (USA, 2nd ed. [1983]).

[5] *Ibid.*, p. 59.

[6] *Ibid.*, The Akathist Hymn, Appendix, pp. 5-6.

[7] T. M. Finn, *The liturgy of baptism in the baptismal instructions of St John Chrysostom* (Washington [1967]), 151. St John took with him the creed of Antioch.

[8] St Basil's *On the Holy Spirit* was originally written to answer a criticism of the doxology which he used in worship: 'Glory be to the Father, with the Son together with the Holy Spirit'. Greek text: Migne, vol. 37, 67-217. A very valuable discussion of the absence of *homoousios* is found in the introduction to B. Pruche, *Basile de Césarée, Traité du Saint-Esprit*, texte, trad. et notes (Paris [1974]). St Basil never explicitly calls the Holy Spirit God, but uses the baptismal liturgical formula as the

basis of his belief in the one triune God. St Athanasius defended his intention (*Ep* . 62 and 63), as did St Gregory of Nazianzus (*Ep* . 58, where he mentions the bishops who reproach Basil for not using the Nicene definition of faith). See also J. N. D. Kelly, *Early Christian Doctrines* pp. 258-263 for the *homoousion* of the Spirit.

[9] St Basil, *On the Holy Spirit*, chapters 6, 9, 11.

[10] Published by F. Conybeare and J. MacLean, *Rituale Armenorum* (Oxford [1905]).

[11] Like the Father in essence, *homoion . . . ousian*. See *Baptismal Instruction*, ed. A. Wenger, Jean Chrysostome – *Huit Catéchèses Baptismales* (Paris [1957]), 119-120.

[12] So St Athanasius says that Christ took 'a human body for the salvation and well-being of man that having shared in human birth he might make man partake in the divine and spiritual nature', *Vita S. Antoni*, 74. 'He was born of a woman . . . in order to transfer to himself our erring generation . . . that we may become a holy race,' *Ad Adelphium* 4, *Contra Ar.* 3:33.

[13] See J. N. D. Kelly, *Early Christian Creeds* pp. 32-37.

[14] See V. Lossky, *The Mystical Theology of the Eastern Church* (London [1957]), 23ff.

[15] The famous text of St Athanasius, 'He was made man that we might become God', *De Incarn.* 54, *Contra Ar.* 2:70.

[16] St Basil denies our ability to know even created things in their total reality of essence, see *Aversus Eunomium* Bk. I.i,c.6 and Bk I.ii,c.4. 'All concepts of God are created idols of God', St Gregory of Nyssa, *Vita Moysis* (Paris [1955]), 82. 'All that we can say positively concerning God does not show forth his nature, but the things that relate to his nature' and 'God is above essence and above knowledge', St John of Damascus, *De Fide Orthodoxa* I,4, PG 94.800A.

[17] 'It is by unknowing that one may know him who is above every possible object of knowledge', Lossky, *op. cit.*, 25.

[18] *The Festal Menaion* and *The Lenten Triodion* contain many of the hymns for the feasts, both translated by Mother Mary and Bishop Kallistos (London [1984]).

[19] Y. Congar, *A History of Theology* (New York [1968]), 28-36.

[20] Cyril of Jerusalem, lecture VI, 9-10. Athanasius, *Contra Gentes* chap. 2-6 and *De Incarn.* 2-4.

[21] E.g., the Council of Jerusalem, 1672, which adopted the later Roman Catholic sacramental theology, see J. N. W. B. Robertson, *The Acts and Decrees of the Synod of Jerusalem* (London [1899]).

[22] F. Gavin, *Some Aspects of Contemporary Greek Orthodox Thought* (London [1936]) and G. Maloney, *A History of Orthodox Theology since 1423* (USA [1976]).

Modern Credal Affirmations

Professor Avery Dulles, S.J.,
The Catholic University of America, Washington, D.C.

Probably no period in history has seen such a burgeoning of new credal formulas as our own. To list and describe the more important statements of faith published within the past twenty years would take as much space as has been allotted to the present article; hence no attempt at enumeration will be made.[1] But to clarify what is being discussed, it may be helpful at the outset to indicate the types of statement that can fall within the scope of these reflections.

Some of the modern credal affirmations are statements by individuals who wish to summarize what they believe in their heart. A number of Christians, especially theologians, have composed short formulas which express either their own personal credo[2] or one which they offer as making the Christian faith accessible to their contemporaries. In this latter category one might place Karl Rahner's three 'short formulas of faith'[3] and others by theologians such as Walter Kasper,[4] Piet Schoonenberg,[5] Hans Küng,[6] and Monika Hellwig.[7]

Not sharply distinguishable from the statements just described are those of a second category: affirmations expressing what Christianity means to some unofficial group or coalition. In this class one might place the credo attributed to Dorothee Sölle[8] and many statements composed by unofficial bodies, such as that recently drawn up by students in the Latin American Biblical Seminary in San José, Costa Rica.[9]

Still a third category comprises quasi-official statements formally accepted by a given church. Prominent in this category would be the Statement of faith of the United Church of Christ (USA),[10] the new creed authorized for the United Church of Canada,[11] the 1967 Confession of the United Presbyterian Church of the USA,[12] and the Confession of Faith of the Presbyterian-Reformed Church in Cuba, published in 1977.[13]

Fourthly, it is possible for groups of churches or their representatives to draw up common confessions expressing what they believe together. This has recently been done in the 'Multilateral Conversation' of six Protestant churches in Scotland, which produced the agreed statement, 'The Faith of the Church'.[14] Very different in scope and tone is the ecumenical 'Affirmation of Hope in Christ' included in the Report of the Faith and Order Commission Meeting at Accra in Ghana, 1974.[15]

The statements alluded to under these four headings, and others that might also be mentioned, differ so greatly from one another in authorship, length, structure, style, purpose, and content, that it is difficult to subject them to any general analysis. Recognizing that nearly any generalizations are subject to challenge on the basis of particular cases, I shall nevertheless make an effort to say something about the dynamics behind the new proliferation of creed-like statements and to describe certain characteristic features of the contemporary formulas, studying them in comparison with the creeds and confessions surveyed in earlier articles in the present series.

The creeds of past centuries themselves fall into many different types. One may, for example, distinguish between baptismal creeds, conciliar (or episcopal) creeds, ordination formulas, and the 'confessions' which came into currency after the Augsburg Confession of 1530.[16] To a greater or lesser extent any one of these classical types of creed serves several distinct purposes. Relying on analyses made by various authors,[17] I find it convenient to list the following six purposes commonly served by such creeds and creed-like statements.

1. *Self-expression*. 'Since we have the same spirit of faith as he had who wrote, "I believed, and so I spoke", we too believe, and so we speak' (2 Cor 4[13]; cf. Ps 116[10]). In view of the bodily and social structure of the human person, people have a natural tendency to express their convictions in intelligible speech. While they can do so in other ways than formal creeds, Paul Tillich had reason on his side when he wrote: 'A church is not quite consistent when it avoids a statement of faith in terms of a creed and at the same time is unable to avoid expressing the content of its creed in every one of its liturgical and practical acts'.[18] As Geoffrey Wainwright reminds us: 'In confessing his faith through the medium of a creed, the believer is expressing his deepest self'.[19]

2. *Doxology*. When believers confess their faith in words, they normally intend to give praise, thanks, and glory to God, in whose presence they stand. According to Gerhard Ruhbach the earliest creeds arose not from situations of persecution but rather 'from the normal situation of the Church, in community worship'.[20] Official creeds very evidently pertain to the public liturgy, especially to baptism, and since the end of the fifth century, to the Eucharist.

3. *Instruction*. The earliest creeds known to us – the ancestors of the Apostles' Creed and the Nicene Creed – were baptismal creeds. They contained summaries of the catechesis given to prospective members of the church. 'Declaratory creeds, con-

ceived in the setting of their original purpose, were compendious summaries of Christian doctrine compiled for the benefit of converts undergoing instruction'.[21]

4. *Witness.* By public confession believers give testimony to the world and invite others to listen, to believe, and to join the community of faith. Some of the short formulas of faith in the NT would appear to have been drawn up as slogans in opposition to paganism and Judaism. Thus a polemic and apologetic dimension is frequently present in credal declarations.[22] Radiating courage, joy, and hope by the way in which they confess their faith, Christians attest to the blessedness they find in adherence to God's word.

5. *Self-identification.* Inasmuch as creeds express the deepest commitments of the community of faith, such statements enable Christians to identify what they have in common and what distinguishes them from non-Christians. Subscription to the creeds has traditionally been regarded as essential for church membership, whereas denial of the creed has been viewed as tantamount to self-excommunication.

Creeds may be called 'integrative' insofar as they make it possible for believers to recognize themselves, and to be recognized as members of the church.[23] To the extent that they are catholic and apostolic, the creeds serve to identify believers synchronically and diachronically with the whole body of Christ. By reciting ancient and ecumenical creeds, contemporary believers intensify their sense of solidarity with the 'cloud of witnesses' who have gone before (cf. Heb 12[1]).

6. *Test of Orthodoxy.* In the early councils, controversies within the church were sometimes settled by the insertion of new phrases into the creed. Nicaea added to an earlier baptismal creed the statement that the Son was 'of one substance' with the Father, and Constantinople added the further state-

ment that the Holy Spirit is 'adored and glorified together with the Father and the Son'. In this way the Arians and Macedonians were excluded from communion. In later centuries it became customary to exclude new heresies by conciliar definitions and dogmas, without further alteration of the creed, but the creed was preserved as a fundamental test of orthodoxy. To contradict it was the most evident sign of heresy.

In the case of suspected heretics or in the promotion of new candidates for orders, additional creeds and professions of faith were drawn up to assure orthodoxy. The profession of faith of the Emperor Michael Palaeologus (AD 1274), the Tridentine Profession of Faith (AD 1564), and the Oath Against Modernism (AD 1910) are quasi-credal statements of this character. This kind of confession differs from the classical creeds in being more local, more time-conditioned, and more heavily doctrinal in content.

In general, the early creeds (such as the *Apostolicum* and that of Nicaea-Constantinople) successfully combine the six purposes listed above. They express the faith of Christians; they are suited for liturgical worship; they serve as a basis for catechetical instruction; they give witness before the world; they integrate Christians into the local and universal church, and they help to discriminate between orthodoxy and heresy. The ancient creeds still retain remarkable power for many contemporary Christians. As classics, they evince a certain capacity to transcend the limitations of their own time and culture. Simple and majestic in style, evocative in images and symbols, they appeal to persons of a vast range of epochs and conditions. They have generated a whole tradition of interpretation and are read today in the light of that tradition. Contemporary theologians still find in these creeds a suitable framework for expounding the essentials of Christian belief.

Why, then, should we be experiencing a proliferation of new statements of faith in our time? One conceivable motive might be to supplement the ancient creeds so as to settle doctrinal points which they had left open. Such was, in fact, a motive behind many of the confessions of the sixteenth century, both Protestant and Catholic, which were intended as more exacting tests of orthodoxy or as self-definitions of new churches (often significantly called 'confessions'). Pope Paul VI, in his 'Credo of the People of God' (1967), had a similar aim in view.[24] He was seeking to recall the official teaching of Roman Catholicism and thus to ward off what he regarded as incipient errors. His creed stands in continuity with the 'ordination creeds', professions of orthodoxy, and confessional writings of the late middle ages and of the early modern period.

For the most part, the recent formulas of faith are quite different in intent. They correspond to two new concerns that have arisen since the Enlightenment. First, they reflect what has been called 'historical consciousness'. Twentieth-century man has a very acute sense of historical and cultural relativity. When reading the Bible or hearing the ancient creeds, our contemporaries often perceive these writings as bound to a strange and alien culture. Thus the ancient creeds are experienced by some Christians as failing to serve adequately the first purpose of the six listed above.

Secondly, post-Enlightenment Christians have an acute sense of subjectivity. They feel that to repeat what has been written by others, especially persons of a very different culture, is to thwart their own individuality. Conversely, they feel that to express their deepest convictions and concerns in their own words is to achieve personal authenticity and to escape from domination by the past.

The motivation behind the modern confession-building movement was profoundly expressed by Dietrich Bonhoeffer, when he wrote in his 'Outline for a Book':

> What do we really believe? I mean, believe in such a way that we stake our lives on it? The problem of the Apostles' Creed? 'What *must* I believe?' is the wrong question; antiquated controversies, especially those between the different sects; the Lutherans versus Reformed, and to some extent the Roman catholic versus Protestant, are now unreal. . . . [T]he faith of the Bible and Christianity does not stand or fall by these issues. Karl Barth and the Confessing Church have encouraged us to entrench ourselves persistently behind the 'faith of the church', and evade the honest questions as to what we ourselves really believe. That is why the air is not quite fresh, even in the Confessing Church. . . . We cannot, like the Roman Catholics, simply identify ourselves with the church. (This, incidentally explains the popular opinion about Roman Catholics' insincerity.)[25]

Many of those responsible for contemporary credal affirmations are driven by the same restlessness here expressed by Bonhoeffer. They want to find out not what someone else believes, nor even what the church believes, but what they themselves really believe, in such a way that they would stake their lives on it.

The new formulas of faith, consequently, differ somewhat in purpose from the classical creeds and confessions. Composed with an acute sense of relativity, they are deliberately correlated with a particular time and place; they purport to express the faith only as it appears from a particular perspective. Consistently with this realization, the formulas are seen as expressive rather than normative. Not only private confessions of faith, but some official church statements accept this limitation. In establishing their Basis of Union, the Congregational Christian Churches and the Evangelical and Reformed Church agreed that their Statement of Faith would be 'a testimony, and not a test, of faith'. As a consequence two authors of the resulting confession of the United Church of Christ have been able to write: 'The Statement of Faith will not be the occasion for any heresy trials. No one will be excluded from the church or denied ordination because of disagreement with it'.[26]

In view of these specific aims, the recent credal affirmations exhibit a number of characteristic traits, verified in most, though obviously not to the same degree in all.

As regards language, they seek to avoid traditional biblical and ecclesiastical terminology and to adhere as far as possible to everyday language. The use of standard church language would, it is feared, undermine the contemporaneity and personal authenticity which are prime desiderata.

In structure, these credal statements display a marked tendency to begin not from faith-convictions (which would imply prior acceptance of the 'faith of the church') but rather from the human situation. They frequently recapitulate the *via inventionis* – the path of discovery traced by an individual coming to Christian belief. Many of these confessions depict in rather sombre terms the predicament of the modern world, with its advanced technology and its political structures, thus making more evident the need for faith and for God.

In doctrinal content, these new statements of faith tend to be far less detailed and explicit than the classical creeds or the Reformation confessions. They usually affirm those elements of Christian doctrine which can be readily correlated with common human experience. For example, Christianity is seen as affirming that human life has meaning and value. God is seen as generous and compassionate. His loving-kindness, rather than his power or justice, is exalted. The Incarnation is celebrated, without precise metaphysical delineation of the 'hypostatic union', as a sign of God's concern 'for us and for our salvation'. The Holy Spirit is not clearly designated as a distinct divine person, but allusions are occasionally made to God as

Spirit and to the 'Spirit of Jesus' at work in the world.

In contrast to the classical creeds and confessions, these new formulas place strong emphasis on social ethics. They seek to arouse Christians to practical engagement in the struggle against social evils such as oppression, hunger, war and the devastation of nature.

The same orientation toward praxis is evident in the eschatology of these statements of faith. Not infrequently they conclude with affirmations of eschatological hope. Whether these affirmations reflect solid convictions on the part of the authors or valiant efforts to stave off despair probably varies from case to case. The content of this ultimate hope is generally left unspecified. The biblical metaphor of the 'Kingdom of God' is freely invoked (in spite of the previously noted preference for common modern language). Only a few of the new confessions make specific reference to personal survival after death or to the glorious return of the Lord. Eschatology is used not so much to evoke trust in the Lord as to arouse Christians to engage in sociopolitical action. Thus according to the Accra statement (which here bears a visible imprint of the theology of Jürgen Moltmann): 'The hope of the Kingdom of God takes on the character of a concrete utopia, that is, an idea of our aim and a critical point of reference for our action in society. This provides us with an incentive to participate in efforts to build a more human social order in the perspective of the Kingdom of God'.[27]

On the assumption that the more common features of the new formulas of faith have here been correctly identified, we may now proceed to some evaluation. On the positive side of the ledger it must be reckoned that these statements function effectively as means of self-expression for their authors. Believers normally profit from the exercise of seeking to put their ultimate commitment into words. As Robert Bilheimer has said, 'the act of confessing forces the person and the community to ever deeper levels of the authentic'.[28] Often the very composition of such statements enables people to discover for the first time that they can sincerely regard themselves as Christians. When composed in collaboration, such statements help to forge a vital sense of community among the co-authors.

The reading and study of modern credal affirmations can be instructive and stimulating to others. Readers can be edified and impressed by the commitment of their contemporaries, and can find in these statements new perspectives on the Gospel. For young and marginal Christians, who have not as yet been fully 'socialized' into the Christian tradition, the new formulas of faith frequently help to mediate the traditional faith of the church, and thus to overcome the sense of alienation from the Bible and the ancient creeds. For those who already accept the creeds, the new formulas may help to interiorize belief. Wolfgang Beinert rightly observes: 'A faith which would relinquish the need to express itself clearly and forcibly in updated ways would thereby condemn itself to disappear'.[29]

In some cases these confessions serve to alert traditional Christians to crucial implications of the Gospel which they might otherwise have overlooked. For example, they may exhibit Christ as the answer to the pressing needs of contemporary humanity or they may call attention to features of contemporary mass-culture that stand in conflict with Christ's message. As one of the principal reasons for confessing faith in God today, Dr Bilheimer calls attention to the prevailing hedonism of our 'consumerist' society. Through new and relevant confessions, he maintains, people can be led to see clearly 'that hedonism cannot be blessed in the name of Christ'.[30]

In particular, many of the recent confessional formulas can help to arouse Christians from an excessive passivity in the face of social and political evils. Calling believers together for committed action, these statements can serve to overcome the twin evils of complacency and despair.

Yet another asset of the new formulations, seen in contrast to the confessions of the Reformation and Counter Reformation, is their generally ecumenical character. Many of them have been composed by interdenominational groups, and even those drawn up by believers of a single tradition tend to focus on aspects of the faith that can be readily affirmed by other Christians, Protestant, Catholic and Orthodox.[31] It is noteworthy that when contemporary Christians try to say what matters most to them, they rarely affirm the distinctive positions of any one confessional or denominational tradition. Thus Bonhoeffer, as quoted above, may be correct in holding that the old interconfessional controversies are no longer central. But it would be premature to conclude that the disputed points are unimportant. It is quite possible that, although admittedly secondary, they may have structural importance for church life and thus be indirectly significant for the individual believer.

Lest the value of the new credal affirmations be exaggerated, their limitations should also be noted. An appraisal may be made in the light of the six purposes of credal statements noted above.

1. As for the first purpose, these statements do indeed express what we must presume to be the mind of their authors, and no doubt of a certain number of like-minded Christians. In many cases, however, they do not adequately express the convictions of Christians who are at home with the biblical and traditional faith of the church, and who regard the consecrated

terminology as important for safeguarding the faith that has been handed down.

2. With a few exceptions, the new credal statements are far less doxological than the classical creeds. Rarely do they seem to emanate from, or be conducive to, prayer and communal worship. This, however, is not universally true. The credal formulations adopted by the United Church of Christ (USA) and the United Church of Canada are suitable for liturgical use, as regards their language and style, though on other counts they might be judged not to substitute adequately for the ancient creeds.

3. Unlike the classical creeds, the new affirmations do not presuppose as their existential context a course of catechetical instruction. They do not attempt to summarize the principal points of biblical and ecclesiastical teaching. For this reason they are perhaps less apt to serve as catechetical instruments, though they readily lend themselves to use in discussion groups.

4. The new formulas vary considerably from one another in tone, but the majority of them can scarcely be described as kerygmatic. Many give the impression of emanating either from solitary individuals reflecting on their personal commitments or from alienated groups dissatisfied with the past and present performance of their church. Where a polemical note is sounded, it may be directed as much against professed Christians as against the forces of unbelief in the world at large. Most of these statements, therefore, serve less well than the ancient creeds to bear confident witness on behalf of the church.

Some of the recent statements of faith, such as those composed by Rahner, are apologetical in intent. They are designed to give 'the kind of witness to the Christian faith that can be really intelligible to modern man',[32] Apart from the question how many people understand Rahner's formula, the problem of reductionism must here be faced. Rahner himself invokes the analogy of 'advertising slogans, party programs, and manifestoes'.[33] Can one faithfully follow this analogy and at the same time present, as Rahner proposes, 'the ancient abiding truth' of the early creeds?[34] Ratzinger, in response to Rahner, contends that while marketing techniques may very well be needed in our modern consumer society, slogans can scarcely transmit the essential content of Christian faith. In Ratzinger's judgment, the new 'short formulas' can serve as a kind of pre-catechesis, inviting to the fundamental decision of faith, but they are no substitute for the creeds, which irreversibly express the content of that faith.[35] Ratzinger's own position reflects a doctrinal rather than a kerygmatic conception of credal statements.

5. On the score of self-identification, the modern affirmations differ somewhat from the ancient creeds. The latter were primarily the work of the church, anonymously composed. They made it possible for individuals to take on a fresh identity by adherence to Christ in the church. The new formulas of the faith, for the most part, do not purport to speak in the name of the church, but rather to express the identity of the individuals or groups who composed them. They are predicated, as we have noted, on a radical pluralism, both synchronic and diachronic, and therefore seek to address only a particular segment of the Christian community for a brief span of time. Very frequently these confessions are designed to express the faith of a persons of a certain age-group, class, nationality, race or political party. For this reason such formulas of faith are deficient in power to integrate believers into the church catholic and apostolic.

This limitation can of course be overcome if the new credal

affirmations are seen as mediating between the tradition and contemporary believers. As suggested above, they might enable some to overcome their alienation and to find themselves at home in the total community of faith. But for this to come about, the pluralism implicit in certain new confessions needs to be moderated. It must be recognized that believers can communicate across cultural and social gaps, and that the Bible and the early creeds can continue to mediate a distinctive and intelligible heritage.

6. As tests of orthodoxy, the modern formulations make no effort to compete with the ancient creeds or the sixteenth-century confessions. This cannot be held against them provided they do not inhibit people from recognizing that orthodoxy ('right thinking') is a real value, and that the human mind, as well as the emotions and the will, needs to be transformed by the Gospel. The authors of some contemporary affirmations seem to exude a certain sense of superiority in being liberated from any concern for orthodoxy. Without approving everything commonly connoted by the term 'heresy trials', one may legitimately claim that sound doctrine is an authentic Christian value – one more effectively promoted by the earlier creeds and confessions than by the majority of new credal affirmations.

As a final reflection, it might be mentioned that no creeds, confessions, or affirmations of faith, whether ancient or modern, can function properly outside a believing and worshipping community. Faith, being oriented toward ultimate mystery, can never be fully reduced to explicit statement. Much of its content is better communicated by liturgy and conduct than by words. Within the community, however, verbal formulations can serve to direct the thoughts and actions of those embarked upon the way. Creeds and confessions are important links between the faithful and the Lord who calls them to himself.

[1] Examples may be found in *ET* 83 [1971-72], 345; 84 [1972-73], 24, 151, 191, 214; 85 [1973-74], 343. For other samplings see *Uniting in Hope: Commission of Faith and Order, Accra 1974* (FO Paper 72) (Geneva: WCC [1975]), 48-88; also the collection in Roman Bleistein, *Kurzformel des Glaubens* (2 vols., Würzburg Echter Verlag [1971]), volume 2.

[2] E.g. the Confession of Faith of René Marlé in *Uniting in Hope*, 55-57; and that of Cardinal Giulio Bevilacqua in H. Schmidt and D. Power (eds.), *Liturgical Experience of Faith* (*Concilium* vol. 82) (New York: Herder and Herder [1973]), 132-33.

[3] K. Rahner, 'Reflections on the Problems Involved in Devising a Short Formula of Faith', *Theological Investigations 11* (London: Darton, Longman & Todd, New York: Seabury [1974]), 230-44. The three formulas proposed in this article are reprinted in K. Rahner, *Foundations of Christian Faith* (London: Darton, Longman & Todd, New York: Seabury [1978]), 454-60.

[4] See the two formulas by Kasper in Bleistein, *Kurzformel*, vol. 2, 100.

[5] Reprinted in Bleistein, *Kurzformel*, vol. 2, 67; also in H. Küng and J. Moltmann (eds.), *An Ecumenical Confession of Faith?* (*Concilium* vol. 118), 91-92.

[6] H. Küng, *On Being A Christian* (London: Collins, Garden City: Doubleday [1976]), 602.

[7] M. Hellwig, *The Christian Creeds* (Dayton: Pflaum [1973]), 96.

[8] In D. Sölle and others (eds.), *Politisches Nachgebet in Köln* [1969], 26ff; reprinted in Bleistein, *Kurzformel*, vol. 2, 118-19.

[9] 'A Latin American Statement of Faith', *Reformed World* 34 [1977], 267-72.

[10] Printed with commentary in R. Shinn and D. D. Williams (eds.), *We Believe* (Philadelphia: United Church Press [1966]).

[11] Text in *ET* 83 [1971-72], 345; see discussion by G. Baum, 'A New Creed', *Ecumenist* 6 [1968], 164-67.

[12] Text in *The Book of Confessions of the United Presbyterian Church in the USA* (Philadelphia: Office of the General Assembly [1967]).

[13] Cf. Robert McAfee Brown, 'Confession of Faith of the Presbyterian-Reformed Church in Cuba, 1977', *Religion in Life* 48 [1979], 268-82.

[14] *The Faith of the Church* (Edinburgh: St Andrew Press [1978]).

[15] *Uniting in Hope*, 28-32.

[16] This fourfold division is taken from J. Ratzinger, 'Noch Einmal: "Kurzformeln des Glaubens". Anmerkungen', *Internationale katholische Zeitschrift* (*Communio*) 3 [1973], 258-64.

[17] Especially useful for this purpose is R. Modras, 'The Functions and Limitations of Credal Statements', in *An Ecumenical Confession of Faith?*, 36-44. See also R. E. Osborn, 'Confession and Catholicity', *Mid-Stream* 16 [1977], 198-205.

[18] P. Tillich, *Systematic Theology* 3 (Chicago: University of Chicago Press [1963]), 190.

[19] G. Wainwright, *Doxology* (London: Epworth Press [1980]), 191.

[20] G. Ruhbach, 'Aspekte der Bekenntnisbildung in der Kirchengeschichte', in G. Ruhbach and others, *Bekenntnis in Bewegung* (Göttingen: Vandenhoek & Ruprecht [1969]), 54.

[21] J. N. D. Kelly, *Early Christian Creeds* (London: Longmans, Green, New York: D. McKay [³1982]), 50.

[22] On the polemical and apologetical dimensions of the NT confessions of faith see V. Neufeld, *The Earliest Christian Confessions* (Grand Rapids, Mich.: Eerdmans [1963]), 30, 64-65, 107, 145-46.

[23] The 'integrative' function of creeds is stressed by Wainwright, *Doxology*, 189-94; also by Modras, 'Functions and Limitations', 40-41.

[24] Text in English in *The Pope Speaks* 13 [1968], 273-82.

[25] D. Bonhoeffer, *Letters and Papers from Prison* (Enlarged edition, London: SCM Press, New York: Macmillan [1972]), 382.

[26] Shinn and Williams, *We Believe*, 16.

[27] *Uniting in Hope*, 31.

[28] R. S. Bilheimer, 'Confessing Faith in God Today', *International Review of Mission* 67 [1978], 148.

[29] W. Beinert, 'Do Short Formulas Dilute the Faith?' *Theology Digest* 22 [1974], 254; digested from his article, 'Kurzformeln des Glaubens – Reduktion oder Konzentration?' in *Theologische-Praktische Quartalschrift* 122 [1974], 105-17.

[30] Bilheimer, *loc. cit.*

[31] See the essays from various confessional standpoints in *An Ecumenical Confession of Faith?* (*supra*, note 5).

[32] K. Rahner, 'The Need for a "Short Formula" of Christian Faith', *Theological Investigations* 9 (London: Darton, Longman & Todd, New York: Herder and Herder [1972]), 117.

[33] *Ibid.*, 120.

[34] *Ibid.*, 122.

[35] 'Noch Einmal', 258-59, 263-64.

The Place of the Creeds in Christianity Today

PROFESSOR WOLFHART PANNENBERG,
UNIVERSITÄT MÜNCHEN

SOME churches use comprehensive confessional statements in order to describe the authoritative doctrinal basis of their teaching. To a certain extent each community of Christians needs a formulation of what distinguishes it from other confessional traditions. But the place of importance assigned to these confessional documents can be very diverse. In the oldest churches confessional documents – although they exist – are not so much considered as the basis, but rather as an expression of the life of the church alongside other such expressions as the liturgy and the canonical structure of its organization. Other churches that came into separate existence at some later point in history are more likely to ascribe basic importance to confessional writings – documents which give witness to their universal claim to Christian truth aand at the same time legitimate the separate existence of such churches after their claims were not universally accepted. Some of the churches originating from the Reformation belong to this category, while others do not attribute such a degree of importance to confessional documents even if they also developed some documents of this kind that serve as reference points in determining their identity.

The doctrinal confessions of the Reformation period and thereafter often refer to the creeds of the ancient church and claim substantial consensus with them. But they are not to be placed on the same level with those creeds. The creeds of the ancient church, especially the Apostolic and Nicene Creeds, did not simply give a comprehensive account of the Christian faith, as the later confessional documents did in their own ways. As they arose from the baptismal catechesis of the church, they could be used as a summary of the faith of the church in the celebration of its liturgy. In many churches today these ancient creeds continue to maintain a firm place in their regular liturgical life, although not all churches attribute such continuous importance to the ancient creeds. But even in some churches that do continue to use the ancient creeds in this way the modern mind has produced widespread opposition and criticism, aimed at both their theological content and their liturgical use. The quarrels over the Apostolic Creed which has troubled the German Protestant churches since the second half of the nineteenth century provide telling examples of such attitudes. Critics of the Creed objected that some of its assertions like the Virgin Birth or Christ's descent *ad inferos* have become obsolete in view of the modern historical reassessment of their biblical foundations and, more generally, because of their conceptual form that the modern mind took to be 'mythological' in character, which applies even to the assertion of bodily resurrection. In a similar way the 'metaphysical' language of the Nicene Creed and of the Chalcedonian Definition was considered irreconcilable with the empirical mentality of modern man. Further, in many cases objections were raised not only against supposedly antiquated elements in the historical creeds, but generally against liturgical imposition of doctrinal formulations upon the personal commitment of the individual believer who participates in the liturgical worship. The act of faith was seen as relating directly to God and to the person of Jesus Christ, not to doctrines about Christ. Given the decisive importance of personal faith and love, the demand for conformity with traditional formulas of doctrine could be suspected of suffocating the vitality of faith and of perverting authentic faith into a new legalism. Such a concern for the utterly personal character of the Christian faith can be traced back to the pietistic movement and to its criticism of purely formal orthodoxy. It contains an important element of truth in that 'confession' in the first place means a personal act of commitment to the person of Jesus Christ. But precisely for safeguarding the authenticity of such faith, confessional statements and credal formulas have been developed in the history of the church. The personal act of confessional commitment and the context of faith which the individual Christian shares with the community must not be divorced. The faith of the individual Christian does not simply stand on its own, and he is not just privately confronted with the scriptures and their witness, but he is related to them as a member of the Christian community, searching in them for the foundational witness to the apostolic faith it inherited. Therefore, in view of the multiplicity and diversity of the biblical witness, the individual Christian almost inevitably feels a desire for a short summary of the Christian faith, and it is not by accident that such summaries have been produced again in our time. Admittedly, the recent fertility in producing modern statements of the Christian faith could also indicate the difficulties many Christians experience with the ancient creeds. However, could any modern formulation actually replace the Apostles' Creed or that of Nicaea? Or do the modern formulations rather contribute to their interpretation and reappropriation?

In its origins the Christian confession was not concerned with doctrines, but with the person of Jesus Christ. The importance and the eternal promise given to such confession were declared by Jesus Christ himself, when he said: '. . . every one who acknowledges me before men, the Son of Man also will acknowledge before the angels of God; but he who denies me before men will be denied before the angels of God' (Lk 12[8ff]. On this saying Hans v. Campenhausen commented by emphasizing that wherever in early Christianity acknowledgement or denial of Jesus Christ was mentioned the impact of this word of Jesus is to be recognized. Therefore, the personal and forensic elements in acknowledging or confessing Jesus Christ must not be obliterated in dealing with the later developments of confessional statements or creeds. Rather, their deepest intention and their ultimate criterion always remain to be found in their meaning for the personal relation of the believer to Jesus Christ. But this does not exclude or denigrate the doctrinal elements that increasingly came to shape the form and character of confessional statements and creeds in the Christian church. The inclusion and growing prominence of doctrinal elements in the Christian confession did not constitute a defection from the original meaning of confession as a personal commitment to Jesus Christ. To the contrary, it was necessary to include such doctrinal elements in order to safeguard the authenticity of personal commitment, since it was meant to relate not just to anything, but to Jesus Christ. It is extremely important to understand the legitimacy of that transition if one wants to appreciate the significance of creeds in the life of the Christian churches to the present day.

An early phase of that transition is discernible in a passage from St Paul's letter to the Romans, where the apostle deals with the close connexion between faith and confession: '. . . if you confess with your lips that Jesus is Lord and believe in your heart that God raised him from the dead, you will be saved. For man believes with his heart and so is justified, and he confesses with his lips and so is saved' (Rom 10[9ff]. Here, the confessional acknowledgement of Jesus is connected with the title 'Lord', which in early Christian thought indicated the position of dignity Jesus occupies as the exalted one at the right hand of the Father. This title is an element of christological doctrine, but at the same time it had its place in the early Christian liturgy where the community acclaimed Jesus as Lord. When the individual joined in this acclamation, it became evident that he (or she) acknowledged the same Jesus Christ whom the apostles and their companions proclaimed: the risen one who is now the Lord and Christ (Phil 2^{11}) – not just a prophet among others, nor some mythical figure, but the Son of God, who 'came in the flesh' (1 Jn 4^2). The joining in the acclamation of the worshipping community became a criterion of the authenticity of the individual's confession to Jesus: '. . . no one can say "Jesus is Lord" except by the Holy Spirit' (1 Cor 12^3). 'Whoever confesses that Jesus is the Son of God, God abides in him, and he in God' (1 Jn 4^{15}). During the period of Jesus' earthly ministry, the use of titles like 'Lord' or 'Christ' had not been essential in the same way, since the person of Jesus was sufficiently identified by his message and by its challenge that demanded decision. After his death on the cross, however, christological titles became crucial in order to identify the person to whom the individual confession relates and the meaning of that confession itself. In this situation, the apostolic proclamation and the acclamation of the community answering that proclamation came to take the place of Jesus himself and his teaching as a criterion of the individual's confession, and as it became necessary to spell out the implications of that acclamation, explicit references to Jesus' resurrection and (with John) to his incarnation entered into the confessional formulas. It is conceivable that in a similar way references to the Father and to the Holy Spirit came to be included in the credal formula. Both of them were implicitly present in the original acknowledgement of Jesus as Lord and Son of God. Thus the triadic scheme of the *regula fidei* emerges, which was developed as a summary of the Christian faith in the baptismal catechesis, but was used for other purposes as well and was finally given a definitive and authoritative form by the early Ecumenical Councils. Along with this so-called 'Nicene' creed, some of the locally or regionally important baptismal formulations of the *regula fidei* survived, most prominent among them the 'Apostles' Creed' of the Roman church that came to be used widely in Western Christianity besides and in place of the Nicene Creed.

In contemporary Christianity the numerous attempts at new summaries of the Christian faith indicate some degree of weariness in relation to the ancient creeds. There is a desire for more modern summaries of the Christian faith, and it is not only a question of language, but also a question of different emphasis in the articulation of the Christian heritage. Such a desire is not necessarily wrong. The text of the ancient creeds needs interpretation, and it has been interpreted in the teaching of the churches ever since their first formulation. But in modern times the need for such interpretation has become particularly urgent. Interpretation partly means historical interpretation. It is only by historical interpretation that the inclusion of a marginal tradition like the Virgin Birth in the creeds becomes understandable today. Within the context of the NT that tradition is indeed marginal, and it obtained its place of prominence in the creeds only because of the anti-gnostic and anti-adoptionist concerns of the early church. Even more marginal in the apostolic scriptures is the image of Jesus Christ's descent into hell or into Hades. But to the early church it became a symbol of the inclusiveness of the salvation. If one is not familiar with interpretations of this kind, it is easy to take offence at such phrases of the creeds. And even where there is no likely offence, as in the notion of the 'communion of saints', the original meaning of the phrase escapes the understanding of ordinary Christians, if no special interpretation is provided. Still more important, however, is the need for constantly renewed application focusing on different elements from those explicitly mentioned in the creeds. Such application that transcends mere historical interpretation has been provided again and again in the teaching of the churches. Why, then, should not the ancient creeds themselves be revised, if not replaced by modern formulas? The answer, of course, is simple enough: No modern formula, excellent as it may be otherwise, could function in just the same way as the ancient creeds do. There is something definitive about these texts that inevitably would be lost if they were changed or replaced by others. This definitive character belongs to the nature of the confessional act and is closely related to the eschatological element in the Christian faith. If one professes one's faith in Jesus Christ, it ought to be done in the face of death and of God's judgment. That means it should be done so that it is never changed again. The Christian confession, of course, is not the only element in Christianity that exhibits such stubbornness and irreversibility. The same is true of the incarnation and crucifixion of Jesus and of his resurrection, and applies to the baptism of the individual Christian. If the confession can be repeated while baptism cannot, still it is one and the same confession. The claim to definitive validity in the unanimous proclamation of the creed by the ancient church, although its wording was disputed over a period of time, shares in the eschatological character of the Christian faith, and therefore it commits all future generations of Christians. Conversely, to the contemporary Christian the ancient creeds present themselves as symbols of the faith of the ancient church. Thus the Nicene Creed symbolizes the conciliar unity of the ecumenical church, while the Apostles' Creed embodies the unity of Western Christianity in spite of all the conflicts and separations that actually occurred within and between the two Christian hemispheres. When contemporary Christian communities join the profession of the ancient creeds within the context of their eucharistic liturgies, they bear witness to the unity of the Christian faith throughout the centuries in view of the future of God's kingdom and judgment. This is the irreplaceable function of the ancient creeds in the life of the churches.

Many individual Christians of modern times, perhaps most of them, would phrase the individual confession of their faith in different words than those of the ancient creeds, if they were asked to express what has become most fundamental in their personal faith. Certain phrases of the creeds would be omitted and other elements would be added that characterize the liberating power of God, of Jesus Christ and of his Spirit in the experience of the contemporary believer. But the creeds cannot be expected to express the individual's faith adequately, nor do they render such personal witness superfluous. They express the faith of the church, and although each individual member of the church is supposed to share in that faith, it may mean different things if applied to different individual situations. Even the language of the creeds itself shows the traces of the particular situation of their origin, as was mentioned before, and those particulars cannot bind the contemporary believer as if he had to consider them essentials of his (or her) personal faith. One can honestly join in the profession of the Apostles' or Nicene Creeds even if one feels obliged to object to some of their phrases, on the condition, of course, that one is ready to identify with the faith of the creed and with the intention even of those phrases that cause disagreement. Here, as elsewhere, the distinction between the intended meaning of a phrase and its historical form is a matter of ongoing interpretation. If the creeds are felt to become obsolete, the churches should take it as a challenge that something more must be done in terms of interpretation. It should never be considered an argument in favour of abandoning the traditional creeds and replacing them by something else. There will always be a difference between a communal statement and the perspective of individual members. This does not demand or justify surrender of the public commitment of the community, but on the other hand sufficient margin for individual appropriation must be granted.

The two ancient creeds symbolize and exhibit the unity of the church in the situation of an otherwise deeply divided Christendom. It is not by chance, therefore, that the ecumenical discussion of this century reconsiders the ancient creeds as a possible basis for ecumenical agreement and for a reunification of the divided churches. In the recent dialogue between the Roman Catholic and Orthodox Churches the church of the first centuries and in particular the early Ecumenical Councils, the faith of which, according to orthodox belief, is epitomized in the Nicene creed, may provide a basis for reconciliation. All the later developments in the period of division concerning doctrine and church discipline should be reconsidered on that assumption as regional developments, interpretations and applications of the faith of the early church as expressed in the Nicene Creed. If the Roman Catholic Church would adopt that model, the entire doctrinal development sanctioned by the Latin synods of the Middle Ages and continued to the present century would be subordinated to the authority of the early councils. It would become a footnote to the Nicene Creed.

Some of the confessional documents of the Reformation period were understood in a similar way to this, even by their authors. Thus the Augsburg Confession explicitly confirmed the authority of the creeds of the early church and applied their doctrine to the disputes of that time. The result was, as in the mediaeval church before, a stronger emphasis on the appropriation in the life of the individual Christian of the salvation achieved by the work of Christ. But all the questions here involved can indeed be treated in terms of an application of the basic faith of the ancient church as expressed in its creeds. As early as in the seventeenth century, therefore, a project for Christian reunification on the basis of the doctrine of the early ecumenical councils could be developed and similar proposals reappeared repeatedly thereafter. Together with the eucharistic liturgy and the episcopal ministry the doctrine of the ancient church could in fact become the basis for a reconciliation between the three major traditions in Christianity – the Roman Catholic Church, the eastern Orthodox Churches and the churches originating from the Reformation. The Anglican Church in particular has always nourished that vision, and although the power of its inspiration could not overcome the particularist spirit in the past, it may still be vindicated. It is hard to imagine how otherwise Christian unity could be achieved.

Not only in bilateral conversations between the confessional families of churches, but also in the WCC the importance of the ancient creeds in the process towards Christian unity has been recognized. Already the doctrinal basis of the WCC of 1948 adopted the christological faith of the ancient church, not *verbotenus*, but in substance. And in 1961 the New Delhi assembly expanded that doctrinal basis to include the trinitarian faith of the Nicene Creed. Still, some of the member churches of the WCC are reluctant to recognize formally the authority of the ancient creeds. Especially some representatives of the young churches from the Third World consider the early ecumenical councils and the Nicene Creed simply as an expression of Hellenistic culture, a particular culture among others, which they do not want to dominate their own culture. Such a concern for cultural distinctiveness and for the inculturation of the Gospel into a plurality of human cultures is certainly legitimate. But on the other hand, cultural autonomy should not be absolutized at the expense of Christian unity. In the past the celtic, Germanic and Slavonic peoples of Northern Europe received the Christian faith from the Greeks and Romans. They received it in the form it had assumed in those cultures, and only in connexion with this process of reception has there emerged what today is known as European culture. There can be no Christian unity without reception of the Christian past as a common heritage, and it is a contingent fact of history that this heritage took its definitive form in the Hellenistic world, after the Greek and Roman Christians themselves had received the Gospel from Palestine and withstood the temptation of abolishing the OT as something foreign to Hellenistic culture. In this way, the Christians everywhere have become heirs of some of the great cultures of humanity. New cultural elements can always enter into this process of recapitulation within the unity of the church, but the church's continuity with its origins must not be disrupted by such dynamics. As the different traditions in Christianity appropriated the ancient creeds in different situations, so it may continue in the present world. Mutual recognition of such diversities of cultural context and application need not prevent agreement in recognizing the common heritage and its authority. To the contrary, such a sense of unity is necessary to enable the adherents of different traditions to respect and appreciate each other and to welcome their diverse contributions as enriching the body of the one church.